Dark Psychology Secrets

The Art of Reading People and Defeating Mental Vulnerability with the Power of Emotional Manipulation

Anthony Secrets

Table of Contents

Introduction

Psychology is the most powerful weapon in the world today, second only to three-stage thermonuclear weapons. It has been employed by the most influential people the world has ever seen, from politicians, businessmen, and even musicians to sway masses their way. Understanding the way, the human mind works is something is the fundamental blueprint to understanding behavior and how to use it to get virtually anything you want from anyone. This knowledge has been highly guarded by those who want to have a monopoly to control the world for centuries. Not anymore! This knowledge is quickly spreading and can now be accessed by the common man with ease. However, not every bit of psychology is currently in the public domain. There are dark secrets about the understanding of the human mind that are kept hidden deep in the pages of powerful books of knowledge. This concept has come to be known as dark psychology. This book aims to bring these heavily guarded secrets to your doorstep. Not only will this book equip you with knowledge about the dark side of the human mind but it will also arm you with preventive measures against those who will try to use this knowledge to manipulate you.

I have specially prepared this book for all my readers in a way that is easy to understand and digest. I have used numerous examples and illustrations to put ideas into a clearer perspective. If you have read my other books, you already know this is going to be another bomb. This book is unique in that it is going to tackle some of the scariest aspects of human nature such as black magic and this means you got to brace yourself for some emotionally-intensive reading. I have not censored any information regarding the dark secrets of psychology in this book. Only those with a strong mind will be able to read the book to the end so grab some coffee and sit tight.

Chapter 1: The Basics of Dark Psychology

Dark psychology is the use of mind control techniques and tactics to influence, coerce and manipulate people into doing what you want. A manipulator will identify weak links in their target's reasoning and use those gaps to sneak in their manipulative thoughts. They understand that there is bound to be some resistance and have since developed new and unique techniques to further their course. That is why we must equip you with the latest techniques used in the secret world of dark psychology. Knowing the fundamentals of dark psychology is not necessarily meant to turn you to a psychopath but these little tricks will come in handy when confronted by dire situations that demand their use. However, the main purpose of bringing these techniques to your attention is for preventive purposes. It will act as a self-defense strategy when you encounter people who want to manipulate or even harm you in a way that benefits them. Those who know nothing about dark psychology stand the risk of it being used against them. Psychopaths and narcissists are fearful of you learning these techniques because they won't be having any advantage over people.

The irony with dark psychology is that the psychopath will use your mind and thoughts in a way that might harm you. Once they take control of your mind, you will become a mere robot that does anything and everything they want. The current world is full of such robots and their masters are the people with the knowledge of dark psychology. This small group of people we are referring to as masters are presumed to possess magical powers. By the time you are done reading this book, you will realize that there is nothing magical about their power. If anything, you will acquire abilities just like theirs and you will understand exactly how they do their thing. There is nothing more humiliating than being fooled by someone you thought you are fooling.

The basics of dark psychology are the fundamental principles used by manipulators in their step-by-step process to control minds. We shall look at these principles from the victim's point of view to make them easy to understand.

Motivating Action and Illusion of Free Will

Motivating action is the attempt by a manipulator to impose their ideas on the target to coerce them to do what they want. The desire to manipulate doesn't just pop up during an encounter with someone. It is a pre-determined and deliberate action. After selecting their target, the manipulator gets their plan underway as soon as they establish contact. Every action and word from the onset takes them a step towards meeting their objective of manipulating you. Manipulators, mostly psychopaths understand that human beings are naturally inclined to give contradictory statements and opinions even when there is evidence. Two people will likely oppose each other once they start giving opinions. A manipulator will take advantage of this rationale to test your thinking before the two of you arrive at a neutral ground. Naturally, the factors of time and patience would force a statement. Such stalemate will not occur here because their pre-determined result is a win situation in their favor. This will appear like a win-win situation for both of you.

Manipulators have mastered the art of turning their ideas into yours. One feature of the relationship between you and the manipulator during the first encounter is that both of you have contrasting ideas and opinions. They will then work their way to your mind and before you know it both of you will be sharing the same ideas. If you arrive at that point and you notice that the ideas are close to their original one, run and don't look back. It takes them less than three meetings to know how your mind works. They will then predict every step you take from your emotions to words coming out of your mouth.

Manipulators this habit of asking mind-provoking questions. If you answer a question the way they expected you would, they smile from the inside. But if you answer it differently, they take notes and modify their strategy until they have your mind at their fingertips.

Concealment

Just like a cheetah waiting to pounce on his prey, a manipulator will conceal their motive from the onset. Even when they meet their objectives, they will still hide the fact that they were achieved through falsehood and deceit. If you will notice this concealment from the following ways:

- They won't ask you direct questions to assert their ideas directly. Their famous strategy is floating an idea to you and when you give a response, they twist and modify it to align with their line of thought.
- They will avoid some questions in a very clever way. They will either pretend not to have heard them or answer them in an irrelevant way. Sometimes the answers they give are too vague to offer any sensible information.

- Your interests are their priority. No one sounds selfless like a person that wants to manipulate you. During your brief or lengthy engagement, everything is about you. They will 'protect' your interests as a guardian angel would. This way, they know they can easily gain your trust.

- Manipulators are very selfish with information. Before a manipulator approaches you, they make sure they have fore-knowledge about the amount of information at your disposal. If you are not well-informed about a specific matter, they will praise your little grasp of the topic to give you false confidence. They will hide the most vital information from you at the same time. Both of you will then come to a consensus using your portion of half-truths to your detriment.

- They will play dumb. Manipulators are some of the best actors the world has ever seen. By the time you are done dealing with one, or let us say by the time he is done dealing with you, you will be left with a memory of a shadow. They will fake everything from their personality to the level of their thinking. You will think you are educating them while in fact, you are walking right into their trap. This further helps them conceal their true motives.

Impairment of critical thinking capacity

Dark psychology aims at taking away the fundamental ability to obey your conscience and guard your interests. Manipulators will hack the process of critical thinking and deny you the freedom of free-thinking. The predator makes your brain bypasses the inspection process by using facts and reason to reduce resistance. They come up with obvious solutions and illustrations for the topic of contention and when you don't get a reason for objection, you won't bother to take the matter into the critical analysis. This is one way by which they interrupt your critical thinking. Another way is by using a more direct strategy that is meant to provoke the target into the thing but then somehow they end up interrupting the thinking process.

To compound the above basics of dark psychology, we are going to use a very short example to illustrate them. This should give you a clear perspective of this discussion. All examples and illustrations we shall be using are not meant to undermine any religion or ideology, neither are they a reflection of the writer's opinions and beliefs. They are entirely for educational purposes.

A cultist would approach you with the intention of making you join their cult. From the word go, they know that you won't accept the offer if they approached you directly. So here is the conversation the two of you will likely hold.

CULTIST: Do you know that there is a God?

YOU: Yes. I know he is somewhere up there.

CULTIST: I can't wait to go to heaven. Nobody else has in our time.

YOU: The dead are in heaven already, the righteous dead.

CULTIST: Yes, but not the real heaven. They are somewhere in between.

YOU: How do you know that?

CULTIST: I have a friend who died for some minutes, he came back after we prayed for him.

YOU: Impossible!

CULTIST: What do you mean impossible? I thought you are a believer; don't you believe in prayers?

YOU: I do, but...

CULTIST: He has been giving testimonies in our prayer meetings.

YOU: oh yeah?

CULTIST: My cousin has been nagging me to take her to hear it for herself. I took her there last week.

YOU: I'm curious.

CULTIST: I can take you too, this Friday.

YOU: Okay.

The above conversation looks very normal from face value. However, there is so much manipulation hidden between the lines. It will take a sharp mind and knowledge of dark psychology to identify elements of manipulation. The cultist has achieved several objectives in less than a minute by impairing your ability to think critically.

He has made you believe there is a god without giving you a chance to clarify the kind of God you two are referring to. The aspect of religion is common to both of you but the finer details are not addressed.

The cultist has perfectly concealed his motive. Normally, a religious person is presumed to be morally upright. If someone starts a conversation and 'God' is in the first sentence, it boosts the level of trust and respect they will be accorded. This is exactly what the cultist has done.

There is a lot of vagueness in the cultist's reasoning. He says that dead people go somewhere in between. This statement is misleading from the beginning, but since he started it with matters to do with faith, he had a free pass. If you had a chance to think critically, you would know that most established religions have a heaven and hell, nothing in between. The mere mention of something between should have been a red flag. But again, he made you believe that it is not entirely their idea nor did he confirm that the source was initially a member of their 'group' before he died.

He makes you think that since you are entitled to know more information about your faith, you wouldn't mind accompanying him on Friday to his 'prayer group'. This looks like your initiative when it is indeed theirs.

At the end of the day, you will join their prayer group to 'hear for yourself'. Before you get there, they will be waiting for you and they know exactly what you will be looking for. They will avail it and you will consume it to your satisfaction. Everything you will be asked to do from that point will be a laid trap. You will be in with both legs before you know it; the power of dark psychology.

These points will summarize the basic features of dark psychology. Keep them at the back of your mind as we shall be revisiting and expounding them in the course of this book.

1. Mind controlling is a motivating action.
2. A tendency to create an illusion that everything, especially the matter of contention, is the idea of the target. This leaves little or no room for objection and resistance.
3. A psychopath or narcissist employs morally questionable tactics that are marred by misdirection, misinformation, and threats.

4. There is a deliberate interruption of critical thinking by the manipulator in ways that don't raise suspicion.
5. The manipulator guards all the interests of the target for as long as their objective is not met.
6. A weak link is created between rational reasoning and objective reasoning to weaken the target's inspection ability.

Chapter 2: Intermediate Techniques

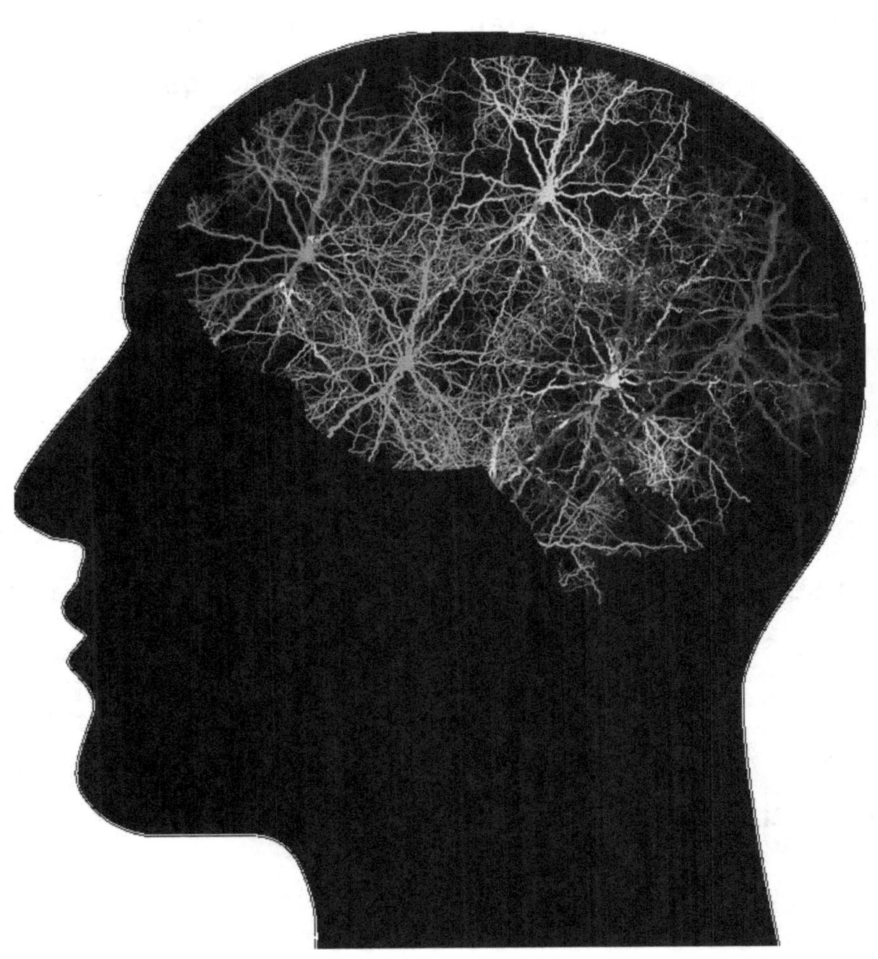

Like I said before, these techniques are not entirely meant for psychopaths and narcissists. They will come in handy at one point in your life, be it in a preventive or any other way. Intermediate techniques are those methods used by manipulators immediately after sneaking into your personal space and gaining your trust. Some of these techniques are discussed below. The techniques are applied to different personalities after assessment by the predator, they are not necessarily uniform to everyone. The techniques are also always undergoing modification by dark psychologists to suit different situations. Politicians, for instance, use prevailing economic and political situations to come up with new tricks to lure voters. Black magicians and cultists, on the other hand, use the most current tragedies to instill fear in their subjects. The techniques are also unique to different communities and cultures. Dark psychologists are experts in applying tactics that suit their situation.

Lies

Psychopaths will always mislead their target in virtually every way. These lies start right from things about their personal lives to their beliefs and convictions. Once they lie to you, you will get confused and end up taking a different route of reasoning. They then use this gap in your reasoning to manipulate you in a way that serves their interests. When a lie is told over and over again, it gradually transforms into a half-truth before finally appearing like a 'truth' to the victim. To get the lie this far, a dark psychologist will ensure consistency in their lying.

Vagueness

A manipulator will not give you the whole story. They make sure that every information they give is lacking the fundamental gist. You won't be able to extract any sensibility from the story. This creates a conducive environment for them to feed you manipulative ideas, ideas that comprise many half-truths or no truth at all. Their stories and ideas are also incoherent. It will take you a lot of time trying to reconstruct the many pieces of information to come up with a story that makes sense. This becomes a delaying tactic as well as a distraction from the main objective by the manipulator.

Feigning Love

Psychopaths and narcissists will go on a charm offensive to lure their victims into thinking that they have their best interests at heart. Anybody would naturally relax in such a relationship and their reasoning is reduced. A level of trust is also built. This reduces objection and resistance by the victim. If someone starts warming towards you for no apparent reason, just know that they are after something. It is a ticking time-bomb that will destroy you. Look out for suspicious affection by someone you barely know or by someone that has not been all that nice before. Normally, they will use and dump you in the most inhumane way immediately their objective is met. It will go as fast as it came.

Unpredictable Moods

People that use dark psychology to manipulate others are always harboring various moods at different times. Sometimes these mood swings are so weird that they not change within short intervals but also have extremities. One minute they are very happy and the next one they will be bursting with anger. Surprisingly, these mood swings are deliberate, it is nothing close to their personality. This is a technique they use to put you off balance. Once they get you started on the wrong foot, it will be difficult for you to detect their next move. Usually, you will find them in their real mood but this changes suddenly to suit the situation, the ideal situation they plan to manipulate you in.

Denial

A manipulator will deny anything that raises eyebrows about their intention. They will assure you that such a thing will never happen. The denial comes every time you talk about the possibility of a negative outcome. If they plan to include you in a dubious business deal, for instance, they will keep refusing the fact that anything might go wrong. They will tell you that nothing wrong will happen whatsoever even when you know it is obvious things don't always go as planned.

Threats

A psychopath sometimes goes to the extent of forcing you to do what they want in an indirect way and warning of the consequences of not doing it. Their tone is characterized by a lot of nagging, shouting and begging. If the situation is dire, they might even resort to physical violence or threaten to use violence. This is normally a desperate measure they apply when they sense that their plan might hit a dead end. Once their target feels threatened, they start doing things out of fear rather than being driven by conscience. This allows the manipulator to exploit that missing link in reasoning to their advantage.

False Accusations

A predator will insinuate that everything that goes wrong is your fault. They will also find fault in virtually everything you do. This is a strategy meant to tear you apart. You will likely end up losing your self-esteem and have feelings of guilt. Again, they have thrown you off balance. They will then create an illusion of perfection on their part. This way, everything they suggest will have a free pass since they have killed the possibility of objection.

Spinning the Truth

Manipulators are experts when it comes to spinning the truth. They will manipulate and twist facts for their benefit. At face value, what they tell you looks like the truth but when you read between the lines, you will notice missing links. They deliberately do this to minimize your level of a grasp on the issue at hand. They also do this as a way of disguising bad behavior. Having succeeded in keeping you in the dark, your mind will be theirs to manipulate at will. Even when you manage to uncover the truth by yourself, they will still have a way of poking holes in it to align it with their version.

Minimizing

Manipulators will deliberately put themselves at a disadvantage when it comes to the level of the grasp of the information. They do this by making errors in their reasoning, just to provoke a reaction from you. If you give a correct line of reasoning about the subject matter, they will taint it with their crooked thinking and that is when your good thinking starts degenerating to their 'level'. They will then manipulate you without a trickle of sweat since you are not the thinker you were a while ago.

Isolation

Psychopaths, narcissists, and sociopaths will isolate the victim from every other source of influence but them.

They will cut you off from your friends, peers, and family. Isolating you gives them a chance to control all information and ideas coming into your mind. This way, they will be able to feed you their ideas from left, right and center. The isolation comes in the form of seminars and workshops where a group of people would be kept indoors for periods that even last months. They are brainwashed and reeducated until they abandon their initial positions. By the time they are released, they will be completely hooked to the manipulator's line of thinking and reasoning. This method has been especially employed by pyramid schemes to nab their victims and turn them into zombies. These are the majority of people that work at the bottom off the pyramid to benefit the minority at the top.

Aggression

Dark psychologists have an over-the-top aggressive habit that is meant to defocus the target. The aggression which comes in the form of anger, threats, and deep withdrawal is meant to reduce resistance and objection. This deliberately manufactured problem makes the victim look for a solution to it first. This distracts them from the real intentions of the prey. If the manipulator acts angry, for instance, the target will first calm them down before paying attention to anything else. In the end, the predator gets a free pass just by distracting the target with the 'anger'.

Innocence

Manipulators are also experts in playing the innocent. This strategy is meant to soften the ground as the target will tread carefully when handling them. Innocence is also a tool they use to reduce resistance. The target will question their judgment every time the predator reacts to a response with innocence. Before you know it, you will be thinking just as they expect and doing what they ask of you.

Sarcastic Comments

Manipulators use this strategy to strip their target of self-dignity and lower their self-esteem. This normally happens when the victim is in the company of others as this is the best time to prick their confidence. Once this is done, the target is robbed of freedom of thinking independently and freely. Hurting their ego will also create fear for the manipulator. The victim will do anything they are told and agree to ideas to avoid worsening the situation.

Flattery

Human beings naturally like being praised. It gives them a sense of self-worth and increases their self-confidence immensely. A dark psychologist is aware of this weakness and will exploit it to the maximum. They will shower the victim with praises and even give credit where it is due. This strategy is magical in earning their trust. Once the manipulator is trusted, most off their suggestions will go unchallenged because the target expects more praise from them.

Avoidance

Dark psychologists will do everything in their power to mislead the target and conceal their true intentions. This is achieved through diversion and avoidance of sensitive topics. As soon as the matter of contention is touched, the manipulator will hastily create a new topic as a diversionary measure. This will happen as its objective is not met. They also avoid tackling matters directly such as giving direct answers to direct questions. Virtually all their responses are irrelevant and vague. It is easy to tell when they are up to something from their avoidance of topics.

Feigning Empathy

Naturally, dark psychologists are among the most heartless and insensitive to the human race. However, they will fake their feelings for you just to earn your trust. They will provoke you into the opening of your problems. They will then pretend to feel bad about your issues while in actual sense they are digging to know your weaknesses. They will then use them against you without your knowledge. You will think they are kind and caring but when they get what they want, they drop you like a hot iron bar.

Guilt Tripping

A manipulator will set numerous traps for their victim to make them feel guilty even when they are the ones at fault. This serves to make the victim more confused and anxious. They will be careful not to do anything that might hurt the feelings of the manipulator. This kind of sensitivity on the part of the victim dispels feelings of selfishness and makes them put aside their interests first. Again, the manipulator win by using the victim against themselves.

Suspicious Generosity

A manipulator will go to greater lengths while trying to please the victim. This strategy involves the flow of expensive gifts like presents, meals, gadgets and sometimes money. This is meant to buy the victim's friendship especially in cases where such friendship would not blossom naturally. Once they win the victim's heart, it is where they will proceed to the mind. It is easy to tell when such kind of generosity is suspicious. The gifts and favors will start reducing as time goes by. Every favor brings them a step to their objective. This comes to an abrupt ending when their objective is finally met.

Endless Games

A manipulator will play the victim's mind in the most gruesome way. This kind of game is characterized by endless lies and promises that never get fulfilled. This technique is meant to buy more time for the predator. It is also a tool used to create a false profile of the manipulator. The lies are designed to align with the expectations of the target and thus give them some false satisfaction. These games will under modifications from time to time to suit new circumstances and situations. A unique characteristic of these games is that they are so accurate and consistent that it becomes difficult to detect them.

Targeting the Victim

Attacks directed at the victim are meant to put them on the defensive. This serves the purpose of diverting their attention from the manipulation. The victim spends more time explaining themselves instead of looking out for the motive behind the attacks. Such attacks and accusations become severe as time goes by until the objective of the predator is met. It is not hard to detect baseless accusations directed to you by the would-be manipulator. Most of the attacks are emotionally driven and in bad faith. If it is happening at work by a boss that does not want you anymore, you will notice that the accusations or attacks are not correctional. They are more provocative and demeaning in a way that will make you look arrogant and disrespectful. The boss will then use this latter reason to fire you, and this gives them an even strong case against you. Technically, they have used you to fire yourself through mind manipulation.

These intermediate techniques do not give dark psychologists enough power to manipulate you. That's why you need to get to know the advanced techniques they use in the next chapter.

Chapter 3: Advanced Techniques

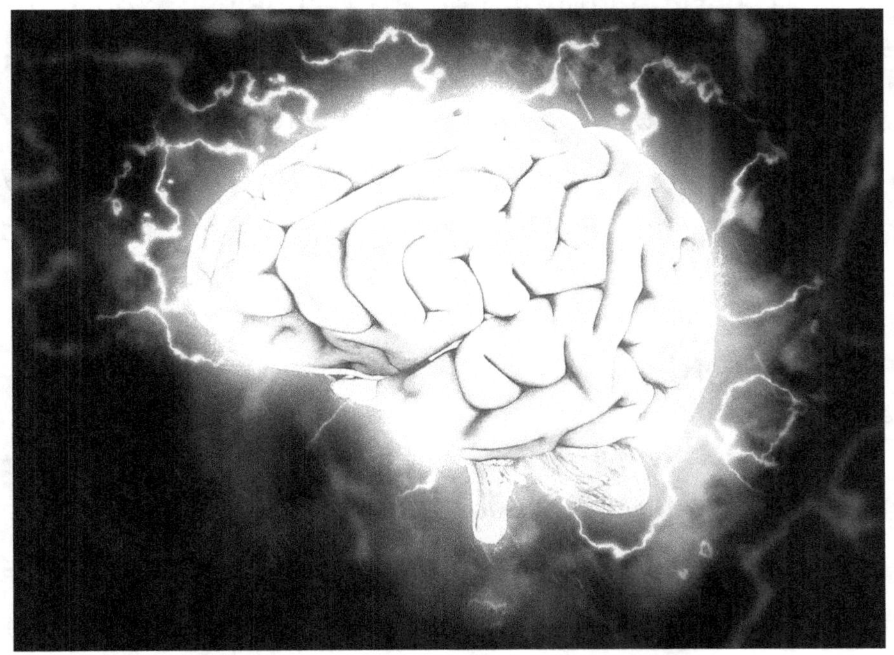

Dark psychologists apply intense and more powerful techniques on their victims when the previous methods fail to work. These advanced tactics are designed to give the target one last blow after several failed attempts. They are more technical and ruthless compared to the previous basic and intermediate techniques. You must get familiar with all these methods, it is only then that you will be or close to be on the same footing as the dark psychologists. These advanced tactics used by psychopaths, sociopaths, and narcissists are discussed below.

Brainwashing

This is a broad and very complicated strategy used by manipulators to bring you to your knees before using you to advance their agenda. The tactic involves complete and total reeducation of the target to shift their moral standing. Technically, it is hijacking the whole personality of the victim without their knowledge. In so doing, a completely different identity is planted on the person to suit the manipulator's interests. Brainwashing has the following characteristics:

Breaks down the old you- this involves the manipulator doing away with your old self. This is done by making you disregard your beliefs and convictions completely. They would find fault in the things you used to believe in and in the way you did things. The loss of principles leaves you exposed and vulnerable. Remember a person's principles are like a compass that shows the direction in terms of reasoning and behavior. If this fundamental ability to stand your ground is taken away from you, a vacuum is created that needs to be filled. You can guess what the manipulator would use to fill that gap.

Crushes the victim's identity- dark psychologists will then make a move at your identity. They will prick your ego by systematically attacking your personality. Prisoners of war have fallen prey to these kinds of attacks where their captors tell them everything they are not and everything they are fighting for. They are labeled slaves of their ideologies. Some of them are even told to their faces that they are not real men or women. This makes you feel worthless and unworthy. A degenerated self-esteem strips you of your dignity and leaves you at their mercy.

Imposes feelings of guilt- a wounded personality and identity become more susceptible to feelings of guilt. The victim now starts hating who they are and become overly ashamed of themselves. Manipulators have perfected the art of fueling these feelings of guilt. They will make their victims believe that it is their fault that they are inferior. They will stress that indeed the victim had a choice about what was good for them but they ended up choosing the wrong things. And since the victim had already been stripped of the ability to defend their identity, they will take the manipulator's word for it. Both of them now team up to attack and blame the victim's old self.

Betrayal- after feeling guilty of their identity, the victim now starts disowning their previous identity. They will find fault in their previous choices even when they could see no fault at all. Everything they have ever done becomes useless and misleading. The victim drowns in their guilt and confesses that they are bad.

Identity crisis- the victim has reached a breaking point. They become completely disoriented and confused. They completely forget who they are and what their purpose is as feelings of shame run through them. At this point, the person would fall for anything that would offer them the slightest consolation. They have lost trust in themselves and are afraid of making any more decisions by themselves. The victim loses grip of reality, they might also sink in depression. Some of them would get overwhelmed and start crying.

A ray of hope- as their target undergoes all the emotional anguish as a result of losing their identity, the predator will be waiting for them to drop dead as a vulture does. They decide to intervene once they realize that their victim has hit rock bottom. They will float the idea of the possibility of salvation once the victim reaches that breaking point. By now they are certain that the victim will not turn down their offer. They see it as the only opportunity to save themselves from sinking to identity oblivion. However, the promise of salvation comes with a long list of conditions to the victim. One outstanding condition will be for the victim to turn away from their former ways. This includes abandoning their previous beliefs and principles. The manipulator presents their ideas as the only way out for the victim. The victim is not given much choice and they have no say regarding their new identity. Everything about the new identity will be sole as designed by the manipulator.

As the brainwashing process nears completion, the target undergoes these stages:

- Leniency is the first stage of salvation. The manipulator starts by offering to remove the victim from that situation of hopelessness, shame, and guilt. If the victim feels some relief from the possibility of being saved, the manipulator then proceeds to state their demands as a favor they need from the victim in return. This stage is also characterized by material gifts and offers such as food, drinks, and money aimed at making the victim feel better. The material offers are also meant to boost the level of trust the victim has on the manipulator.

- The second stage is the compulsion to confession. Here, the manipulator makes their subject see the possibility of helping themselves with only a little help from them. The dark psychologist motivates the victim to assert their desire to come out of their situation and build a new self. Having been presented with the choice of helping themselves, the victim feels obliged to right their past wrongs. They also feel the need to not disappoint their 'savior' who have volunteered to 'help' them out.

- Channeling of guilt becomes the third stage. Here, the manipulator attaches the guilt the victim has been feeling to their old self. The victim is not able to explain the origin of the feelings of guilt at this point. And this is where the manipulator comes with their dubious explanations. In the course of these explanations, a contrast is created between the old set of beliefs and the new ones. The victim's old beliefs will be used as the scapegoat for all the suffering the victim has been undergoing. The new set, on the other hand, will be portrayed as a ticket to a better future full of glory.

- The fourth step involves releasing guilt. The victim is now convinced that their old set of beliefs are the cause of suffering and that they are ready to let go of them. At this stage, the desire for a new identity is unstoppable. The victim has no second thoughts about the change they are about to execute. The level of brainwashing has become so severe that they don't stop to think if there is something good in the old self that needs to be carried along to the new identity. They also don't analyze the new offer critically to see if there are any shortcomings associated with it. All they want to do is bury the old self and become something else, completely new.

- The person starts rebuilding themselves. After doing away with the old identity, the victim embarks on rebuilding and restructuring themselves according to the manipulator's manual. The instructions in that manual are supposed to suit the predator's interests 100 percent. The victim has no share in the new person they are building. They are just serving robots with the manipulator as their master. The victim feels that they owe the manipulator for fixing their brokenness. This is enough reason to do anything they are asked without objection. The manipulator sees this as a perfect opportunity to implant their version of ideas in the victim with certainty that there won't be any objection.

- The last stage of brainwashing is harmony with the new self and starting over. The new identity comes with calm and comfort for the victim after a period of emotional disturbance. The dark psychologist makes this appear like the victim's choice and initiative to build a new self. Technically, the choice was made for them when the old ways were demonized and the new ones praised by the manipulator. The victim would naturally choose the latter but the choice was clinically imposed on them. After finding comfort in the thought of following this new path, the victim embarks on a journey to put the new beliefs into practice. The manipulator becomes their new 'mentor' as they start the journey.

Metacommunication

This is a strategy used in the world of dark psychology where the manipulator uses a stream of subliminal messages on their target. These messages are implanted in the subject's mind during long indoctrination lectures. The messages in the form of short statements and slogans are repeated over and over until they stick in the victim's mind. The human mind is programmed to recall and familiarize more with repeated things. In such lectures, most of the contents are unrelated to the manipulator's aim but they serve as a way of relaying a message contained in the subliminal remarks. The message can be coded or just bare depending on its sensitivity. For example, a black magician would use words like 'for nothing happens without blood sacrifice' severally in the middle of their chanting to insinuate that the target needs to familiarize themselves with the issue of blood sacrifice. If these words are repeated over and over again, your mind will stick to them despite having heard many more words in the chant. This is meant to wire your brain into giving more thought to the words. Once you start entertaining the thought, your curiosity will be awakened. You might start considering the words every time you are faced with a dire problem that needs to be solved immediately.

Politicians have also created slogans to advance their agenda. The world of dark psychology uses such slogans to manipulate and influence masses to their advantage. The Nazis, for example, created slogans that fueled their anti-Semitic agenda before and during the Second World War. Every time such slogans were used in public meetings and rallies, feelings of hatred would run high among the crowds. People would then leave the meetings with charged emotions and end up harming those people whom the slogans targeted. This is the reason some of those slogans and accompanying gestures such as "hail Hitler" came to be banned by governments of the world after the war was over. They caused more psychological harm to the victims in greater numbers than the ones harmed physically.

Disinhibition

This tactic is used by dark psychologists to control the minds of their subjects by making them look inferior. It is a technique that is mostly used by a cultist. The subject is encouraged to obey and follow like a child. The manipulator elevates themselves to a more superior position to instill fear rather than command respect. The victim is presented with two options when it comes to obedience; obey and benefit from it or refuse and suffer the consequences. To give more weight to this rule, the manipulator devices ways of punishing those who don't obey them and even goes to the extent of punishing them to drive the point home. In some religious settings, coinciding tragic events are used to instill fear on the masses and force them to do certain things. This normally happens when they want to extort the subject. They will wait for a misfortune to befall you and then use it to advance their agenda. They would tell you things like, 'your child got sick because you have refused to give a certain amount of money'. This statement is accompanied by a 'solution' that also serves as a warning; 'if you give the money, the child will get well, if you don't, and more misfortunes will come your way'. This obedience of a child allows the manipulator to make demands on you at will for as long as they want.

Rigid Rules

A manipulator will set extremely strict conditions and rules that can only be compared to a dictatorship. These rules are designed to guide the target to each of the laid traps. Bending these rules has the potential of jeopardizing the whole process so they will avoid it at all costs. The unbending rules are also meant to create limited time for thinking and action by the target. They are left with the easier option of following the rules as they are. Every time the victim tries to negotiate about changing or modifying the rules, they either get ignored or threatened altogether. Sometimes the bureaucracy attached to changing the rules is too hectic and weary that the target would normally give up before making any significant gains. Corrupt government officials, for instance, would come up with a complex channel of communication or network of financial flow that would make it difficult to trace looted funds. Since the human mind is susceptible to fatigued, the victim gives up after just a few attempts. Rigid rules should always be a red flag whenever you come across them. They are likely masking a form of manipulation.

Sleep Deprivation

It is funny how people respond to things in their sleep irrespective. I once asked a friend that was half-asleep if I could borrow their phone. The sleep was becoming so heavy that he just murmured a 'yes' to my request. Two hours later he woke up and found me using the phone. He asked, 'who gave you permission to use my phone?' I answered, 'you did'. He insisted that he didn't give out permission. I smiled and gave the phone back. There is a tendency for the brain to refuse to work properly when someone is asleep or wants to sleep. The brain's activity slows down when someone wants to sleep. It is even worse if you have not had enough sleep for a long time. The level of the brain's refusal to think can be compared to a total shutdown. A manipulator understands this phenomenon very well and will exploit it to the maximum. They will approach you when your brain is less active due to prolonged lack of sleep. They will then manipulate your thoughts and implant their ideas on you without much resistance. They might even go the extra mile of engaging you in some mental or physical activity that will make your brain even more tired. The mind is more vulnerable at this point.

Blackmail

This is an act of coercion that involves the use of threats to achieve a certain objective. A manipulator will target the victim's property, money and threaten to harm them or people that are close to them. This can also be viewed as a form of extortion. Dark psychologists will use this strategy to force their way into the mind of the target. Before resorting to blackmail, it means the manipulator has exhausted almost every other method but seems to have hit a dead end, so this becomes a desperate move at the target. When at times the target doesn't give in to the demand, this desperation pushes the psychopath to make real their threats. In a way, this is a win situation for the target even though they might have incurred losses of property or having their loved ones harmed. Terrorists and criminals have been known to employ this technique to manipulate their victims. Smart governments that have noticed this kind of manipulation have come up with policies of zero tolerance to such manipulation. The United States government, for example, has a slogan, 'we do not negotiate with terrorists' even when those terrorists are holding hostages. This method has proven to be effective in the fight against terrorism since not giving in to their demands defeats their ideology. Imagine how many attacks and hostage-taking situations would be occurring if their wishes were granted every time they do that. My advice to you if someone tries to blackmail you is that you'd rather lose that property than lose your freedom of mind forever.

Familiarizing yourself with these advanced techniques used in the world of dark psychology will equip you with the knowledge and skills to guard yourself against mind control and manipulation. Like I said before, these skills are not meant to train you to be a psychopath but they will come in handy when the situation demands.

Chapter 4: The Secrets of Dark Psychology Used and Developed by the Secret Services

There a common form of psychology that was developed and is being used several secret services globally. This form of dark psychology is known as spying or espionage. This act can be described as the process of gaining access to information that is very confidential without authorization from the party holding the information. This act is done by people known as spies who aid organizations to unearth secret information.

People who commit spying are given orders for their actions from a company, government or independent operation. The process can be termed as a clandestine operation from its description. There are some cases that spying can a legal tool to help in enforcing the law. However, there are some instances it might be unlawful leading to punishment by law. The process of espionage entails the gathering of information intelligently from sources that are not disclosed. This form is mostly a part of governments or commercial institutions. However, this term is commonly related to a country spying on actual enemies or potential enemies because of military purposes. Industrial espionages are a common phenomenon that involves spying operations.

There is always an easy way out for gathering information which is used by secret services. The most effective way entails an individual infiltrating the ranks of the sports organization. This can be a good description of the work a spy agent does. In return from the task, a spy agency can give information of actual information on the strengths and size of the target. A spy can go a notch higher to finding any form of dissident within the target and use it to defect or a tool to acquire more information. Spies are known for stealing technology during moments where the crisis is experienced.

Several countries and organizations have invested heavily in counterintelligence. The reason behind this action is to be able to tackle spying from other parties. Several nations across the globe have stringent laws that are enacted for anyone who is caught or found guilty for spying. These penalties are often severe to a guilty party. On the other hand, the process is very beneficial to several countries or institutions. It is because the information gained through spying is very important to several forms of success.

History of Spying

There are several people or acts that are widely targeted by secret services with the use of spying. These common activities include illegal drug dealing and terrorism. A country that has seen heavy spying on it is the United States of America. It is because it has been able to charge approximately fifty-seven defendants who were attempting to spy for China. This means is a wide target for espionage from several people and countries. However, the phenomenon can use to depict its investment in spying as a country with huge interest tends to have a huge number of spies to protect it.

Secret services such as intelligence servers or intelligence units, value certain forms of intelligence collection techniques over others. A good depiction can be used by the former Soviet Union. It had a huge preference for gaining information from human sources over that from research from the open sources. Another example can be elucidated by the United States of America. This country has put its major focus on several technological methods such as IMINT and SIGINT. Officers in the political or military sections in the Soviet Union were judged by the figure of agents they had recruited.

Targets of Spying

Spying agents are always required to have undergone an intense period of learning. This makes them become trained experts in the fields they are targeted to venture in to. The process of training spies is very important because it helps them to differentiate important information from fake or unimportant information that is advantageous to their agencies. One of the important stages in espionage is being able to identify the correct target for executing.

Therefore, there are several areas that espionage can target. These areas include:

1. Natural Resources

The area includes identification and assessing of areas with strategic production of natural resources. This includes areas producing food, materials or energy. The spy agents have a specific positioning in this area. They are mostly situated as bureaucrats who administer the same resources in their home countries or organizations.

2. Popular Sentiments

There are several sentiments that are always expressed in the current social world. These sentiments can either be pushed towards foreign or domestic policies. Their targets are diverse ranging from different social classes and backgrounds of people. This edge of the target has a very small niche of recruits to be able to perform the tasks with fines. This niche includes post-graduate students, sociology researchers or journalists.

3. Strategic Economic Strengths

The field of economic strength can rage from a variety of sectors. These sectors include infrastructure, research, manufacture, and production. This target also has special people who are recruited to bring about success in the spying process.

4. Military Capabilities

There are several factors that spied when the target is the military capabilities of the other party. These factors include the other party capabilities and intelligence on the offensive, maneuver, naval, defensive, space and air. These forms of spy agents attend schooling in military facilities that train and educate military espionage. These people are then posted to their area operation with new identities. This cover identities they are given help them to minimize the extents of prosecution in events they caught.

5. Counter Intelligence

During this process, the same organization spies itself. Several factors are always examined during this process.

Some of these factors include the breach of communication confidentiality internally and search for moles or defectors within the organization. The process is very delicate as it needs some level of fines. A slip may mean the downfall of a country or an organization because of the impacts spying has on the public eye.

Method of Spying

Clandestine Human Intelligence

This form of spying involves the collection of intelligence from humans as the sources. The process involves the usage methods that are of clandestine espionage nature. These people who are targeted as sources of information work in different sectors of the world under the intelligence community. Quintessential spies are very common to people since they are known as professional agents. They have very unique roles which include collecting intelligence, handling couriers and related people in the service and handling organization intelligence such as securing communications. These spies can either be the people being recruited to work or the people recruiting others for these jobs.

There certain situations where the person supervising the recruitment process is the same individual recruiting people. Huge secret services have a large composition for its success. The composition includes multiple spying levels, supervisors and people who offer support. These systems that carry out spying are always organized themselves as cell systems. This makes the person operating as a spy to only know the people he or she shares in the cell. A spying individual is certain to know to include the external case officer and the leader of the cell. They are then equipped with an emergency strategy that they can use to get out when in a heated moment. This is done without an individual knowing people from the other cells. This trick used by secret services is known as compartmentalization that is critical in retaining the urgency information and minimizing damage.

Process of Becoming a Spy

For an individual to become a great spy he or she is supposed to improve his or her mental capabilities. He or she is supposed to be able to go through a crowd without getting noticed, becoming an eavesdropping technique and other techniques used in trade. These qualities are very critical to help an individual to be able to establish a basic protocol that helps in making these spying missions successful. The process is split into three parts for an individual to be able to understand the process deeply.

Part One: Becoming a Spy Material

1. Getting gutsy

There are several factors that an individual is supposed to be able to look at some things while spying. It is because one will be tasked with going to a danger zone. These places are always filled with several variables and factors that are unknown. Therefore, an individual is supposed to be able to push him or herself to situations that seem new to him or herself. This will help him or her not to get phased out by anything spying process.

2. Getting smart

This process entails more than what common people are used to reading or watching. An individual is supposed to be super-intellect in order to be able to acquire the desired form of information. It is the reason why the process is termed as intelligence gathering. Therefore, spies have a varied expansive knowledge in the field they choose to venture in to. This knowledge is supplemented by other forms of knowledge in the related fields he or she is assigned in.

3. Getting creative

People who are good spying are very good at being creative. It is because; an individual is highly advantaged when he or she begins to rely on him or herself to find answers to several issues. There are several instances that secret services do not equip their spies with gadgets. The reason behind this action is to be able to process and analyze situations on their own using the disposable resources around them. This process entails the simple form of a person being mindful and thinking outside the box. Anything through a keen eye can be a clue or vital information.

4. Getting a day job

A spy will certainly need a cover to be like a normal person. Having a day job helps to cover the true habits, nature, and intentions of an individual. Therefore, spies tend to enroll in jobs that they are best in or have a clue in. This helps them not to land into problems simply because they do not their tasks. A failure in such can lead to a rise in eyebrows. However, this does not entail an individual going to do overtime roles frequently.

5. Getting in good shape

Physical confrontations are something that spying tends to avoid all costs. However, staying fit always comes in handy during certain situations. These situations include tailing someone or when in a position to make quick getaways. Therefore, it is a common occurrence for a spy to hit the gym, have run or making walks for long distances. They also go a notch higher to practicing self-defending techniques such as karate if they do not hail from a military base. The process of getting in shape also includes minding mental strength. A spy is supposed to be able to react calmly yet swiftly with the mind while making his or her choices.

Part Two: Getting Unnoticed

1. Hiding in plain sight

One of the most important objectives to be achieved by a spy is to be able to blend in with people. An individual is supposed to have a good dress code that is not extravagant. He or she can go ahead to having clothes that are suitable for every event he or she attends. There are sessions he or she is supposed to dress officially and there will be occasions or situations that he or she will be required to dress casually.

2. Keeping one's gear to a minimal

The importance of observing this factor is because it helps an individual to be more mobile. An individual is supposed to carry items that are essential for the mission. An individual is not supposed to unnecessary weapons that can unravel his or her identity. Therefore, he or she will be required to improvise during certain situations.

3. Participating in activities around

There are several activities that people participate in a spy. He or she is supposed to be able to blend in and participate. However, it is always best if a spy does not overdo in his or her participation. The choices of activities to participate in are supposed to be simple and obvious.

4. Deleting oneself record from the internet

The aim of this step is to enable an individual to stay in incognito. It won't be a good show if pictures or profiles of a spy can be pulled up easily from the internet.

However, it is okay to be online if it is done in a careful manner.

5. Not running to the crowd

The act of running to the crowd or being rowdy is not advocated during the spying process. It is because an individual can blow his or her cover by attracting attention from people.

6. Not being nervous or reacting if one is seen

Being a spy entails an individual being cool so as to avoid several suspicions. However, there are a certain situation is prone to be tensed or worried. If one is seen or noticed, he or she is not supposed to leave or react in a questionable manner. The mind of people can be a gullible thing; he or she is supposed to swiftly change the tune of emotions in public.

7.   Knowing when silence is necessary

Having a sound environment around a person draws away several forms of attention. This includes having a good form of breathing, having pieces of clothes that do not make noise and most importantly being a smooth talker.

8. Getting a disguise

This part is not necessary and an individual does not have to be perfect at it. There are moments when spying; looking outrageous will help to reduce suspicion from people. This includes acts such as having big glasses or ugly sweaters.

Part Three: Usage of Spying Techniques

1. Starting of eavesdropping techniques

It a very hard act pretending that you are not paying attention to a conversation nearby. The process becomes more difficult when there are no people around during such moments. During these moments it is a hard task for someone to distinguish the voices of people talking while blending in with people for the first time. The technique of eavesdropping helps an individual to solicit information even in sloppy situations.

2. Learning how to read lips

There are certain moments a target of a spy can be several meters away or there might be noise. These two situations can make an individual not to hear what a spy target is saying. Therefore, he or she is forced to know how to read lips. This makes it possible to follow conversations among people.

3. Mastery of lying and being able to detect lies

Intelligence an individual is able to gather during the spying process won't be important if it is full of misinformation. The process of comprehensive reading of people will help an individual know how to read the body language. There are certain body languages such as the way of standing, eye movement, and arms positioning can be critical.

4. Learning how to tail a target

Humans are very mobile beings; therefore, people rarely stay still for a long time. A spy is tasked with knowing the movements of his/her target often. During tailing a target, it is always better for a spy to have a backup plan.

5. Being able to steal things without getting caught

The process of being a spy requires an individual to become a good thief. There are several moments an individual will be required to steal evidence that have vital information. These moments require actual finesse from an individual because their moments the act will be done in broad daylight or during dark moments. The situations that present with an opportunity to steal are always grabbed with open arms. This process can be initiated by trying stealing little things such as pens and upgrading.

6. Being good and updated with technology

The process of spying does not only entail an individual being on the field with binoculars. There are moments an individual is presented with a chance to use technology while on duty. Having a good knowledge that is updated on technology is very advantageous to a spy. It will help him or her to be able to save time in accessing certain forms of files from a target.

7. Improving one's memory

The intelligence an individual gathers during the session of spying won't benefit an individual if he or she has a mind related to the steel trap. Therefore, an individual is supposed to be able to have a good memory. There are several methods a person can improve his or her memory while spying. Activities such as solving puzzles and games such as chess help to work the brain and strengthen one's memory. This also helps an individual to become more observant of things going on.

Chapter 5: Body Language and Microexpressions

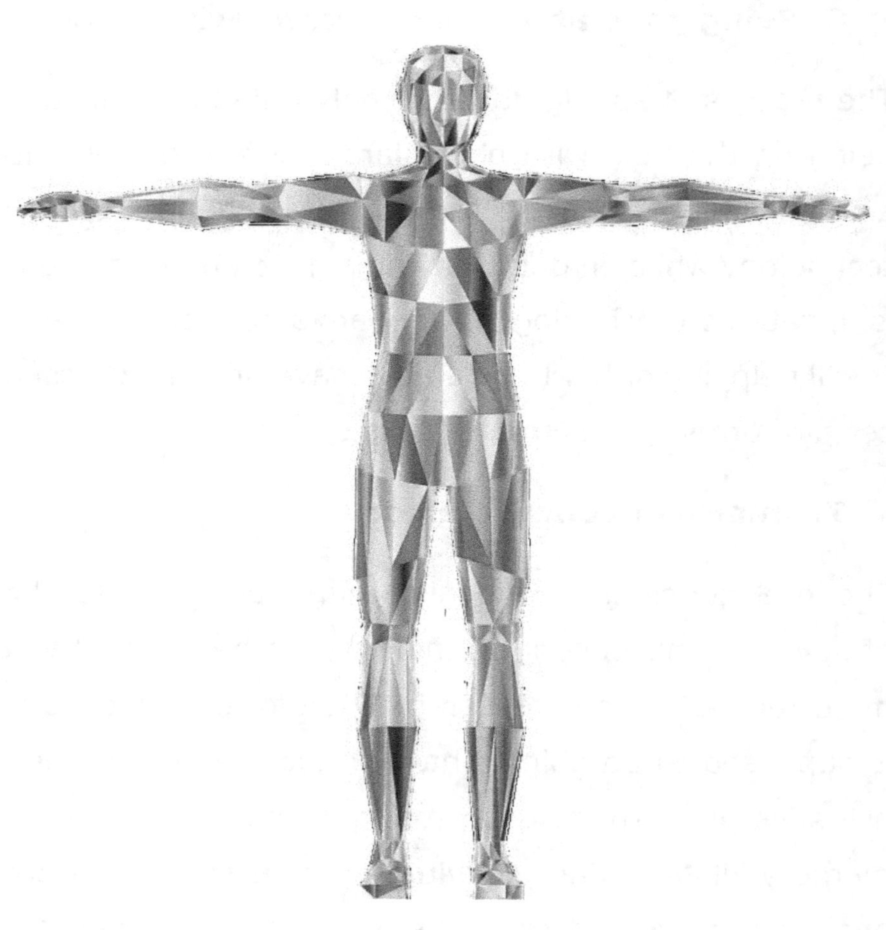

Microexpressions

This chapter focuses its radar on the various types of body language and micro-expressions, their meanings and effects. When one is faced with difficulty during a conversation, they tend to do things as a result of the discomfort. For instance, when you want to know an individual is not telling the truth, often you will see them fidgeting or making some signs with the eye that means that the person is not comfortable with what they are being asked about. This is what is referred to as micro-expression. They are the small signs that an individual exhibits when they are being faced with questions that tend to expose them. Insecurities are usually the main generators of these micro-expressions. Microexpressions can also be referred to as micro-momentary expressions. This is because their effect is not lasting and that it occurs for a short period of time only. They come around in flashes and disappear in a jiffy. A person who is keen enough is one who will be able to realize. As human beings, we have the tendency to hide our emotions when we have the tendency of revealing our innermost emotions through our facial expressions. This is how we communicate when we are in a position of turmoil. These behaviors often occur without our know-how. We often do not wish to exhibit what we feel. This because human beings have time and again been attributed to betrayal. It is by this fact that we will conceal this feeling. In relation to the information already mentioned above, we can deduce that a micro-expression is the inborn feeling of involuntariness and voluntariness to express a particular emotion. The body is overwhelmed with emotions that it wants to let out but the mind is not willing to discharge these emotions.

There are a number of ways you can be able to deduce micro-expressions in another person's face. The face is the main medium that forms a basis when detecting these micro-expressions. The muscle may also apply but the face cannot lie. Sudden changes in the human face will let us know what the other party is experiencing. When we relate a particular subject to someone, the reaction will always be denoted by their facial expressions after you have mentioned it. The person wants to respond but they cannot. The feelings of response are written all over their faces. Apart from micro-expressions, there exists a different type of expression known as macro-expressions. These are the obvious feelings of sadness or laughter that appear on an individual's for a longer period of time say two to four seconds. They relate to what an individual is putting across. This is opposite to micro-expressions as micro-expressions tend to conceal what an individual would not put across. In order to understand the non-verbal expressions of an individual, one needs an acute comprehension of facial expressions.

Various types of Micro-expressions

As earlier on discussed, the face is the biggest media that is used to channel these micro-expressions. This is because it lays the foundation for the five senses that an individual has. Any response to certain stimuli will be seen in the face. The various types of micro-expressions include:

Expression of Surprise

The surprise is a feeling that is exhibited when you are encountered with events that you had the least expectations of their occurrences. This could be the first time that you are seeing a particular thing. It may also be hat you have never witnessed a certain turn of events. In order to deduce that one is feeling surprised, you have to focus on particular key pointers. They are often facial expressions. They include:

Heightening of the eyebrows in a manner that they seem to be curved. This will, in turn, cause a stretching effect to the skin below the eyebrows. The forehead will now start to wrinkle owing to the rise in eyebrows. The whole eye socket is exposed to the extent that the white part of the eye is seen. The lower jaw of the mouth will drop and as result teeth will part. The degree of surprise varies according to the information dispensed.

Expression of Fear

Fear comes as a result of phobia that something might cause harm. The harm might not be necessarily direct but it can also be indirect. The phobia that something might cause harm to your loved ones may also take a toll on you. You are in a situation whereby you are in anticipation that something ill may happen. The result of this occurrence will not sit solemnly with you. In order to detect fear, there are various pointers that are key. For instance, your eyebrows pull together resulting in somewhat a straight line. The forehead will exhibit wrinkles in a manner that is discrepant to the one under feeling surprised. Here, your wrinkles will surface at the center of both eyebrows. The eyes are in a moment of strain since the upper covering of the eye is elevated while the lower covering sits at rest. The eye socket is not wholly exposed since it is only the upper part of the eye that is exhibiting the white matter. The mouth remains open while the lips align themselves perfectly along the teeth line.

Expression of Disgust

Disgust is an expression that is exhibited when an individual is not feeling what you are showing them or telling them. Disgust can be as a result of something you do not like or something that irritates you. Take for instance you see somebody's puke, you will be inclined to feel like you are almost puking yourself. This is because what you feel does not rest solemnly with you. The various pointers to disgust include: The upper eye-lid tends to be raised as a result of being aroused. The lower lip also remains raised thus tightening the grip of the mouth. The nose's position is distorted as a result of raising the mouth. This, in turn, makes it be wrinkled. The cheeks are also raised as a result of raising the lower lip of the mouth. Since the upper eyelid is already raised, lines start to form below the lower eyelid.

Expression of Anger

This is a common expression to most of us since we tend to be annoyed almost every day. Anger comes about when somebody performs an action not necessarily to you that triggers your emotional response. The act or omission may be to your loved one or to a disadvantaged group of people. The cause of anger varies from one persona to another due to experience issues. The key pointers to this type of expression include The eyebrows lower and pull together because you are experiencing a feeling of anger. When the eyebrows pull together, they form lines in between the eyebrows. This has an effect on distorting the lower lid of the eye which in most instances will be shaking at this point. The eyes are focused on one single gaze that they hold on to for a period of time. When it comes to lips, they adopt various positions according to the individual. They may be placed together firmly or shaped in a manner that exhibits a square. The nostrils are either dilated or not depending on the rate of breathing.

Expression of Happiness

Next, to anger, the expression of happiness is one of the most common expressions that we have. People will always be amused when something is hilarious. This is a feeling that you cannot conceal. Often it comes about as a result of seeing or visualizing something amusing. This can be as a result of sentiments expressed by someone. Detecting this feeling is not a subtle as the others maybe. The pointers include: the lip corners forming a crescent shape because they are pulled back upwards. The enamel is exposed and somebody may be able to denote white. N enormous wrinkle forms connecting the nostril to the outer lip. The cheeks are pulled upwards due to the formation of somewhat a smile. The lower eyelid reacts according to the degree of happiness. It may exhibit wrinkles or remain shaken. It should be noted that there is a big difference between the expression of real happiness and fake. Fake happiness concentrates largely on the exposure of teeth. A person may be smiling but is not happy.

Expression of Sadness

Sadness comes about as a result of feeling weak or inferior to somebody. Sadness has its roots in the feeling of being annoyed yet you cannot do something about it. Often this is what makes people sad. The feeling of sadness can be denoted by the following pointers. You will often find that the inner corners of the eyebrows pull together inwards and then upwards. Below the eyebrows, the skin there appears to be in a triangle like shape. The lips are drawn downwards in that their corners are pulled downwards. Normally the lower lip is often drawn outwards in a manner that suggests you are lonely.

Expression of Contempt

Being in contempt refers to an emotion of superiority towards someone. For instance, you can be in contempt of court when you perform acts that are not acceptable by the court. The feeling of contempt is often denoted by the mouth. This is characterized by the escalation of one side of the mouth while the other side rests.

Body Language

For effective communication to ensue, the art of communication needs to be accompanied by some gestures. These gestures are body movements that tend to facilitate the driving of a particular message home. There are various gestures that vary from one communication to another. In order to comprehensively get the information, the gestures have to be in unison with what you are trying to put across. For instance, you may be instructing someone to do something whereas your gestures tell a different story altogether. When we are using body language, most of the time we are not aware of it until it. You will see your hands moving without your instruction. This is what happens when another person is communicating. You will read the body signs without your know-how. The limbic brain is what controls these movements in the unconscious state. In order to communicate effectively, one needs a clear understanding of the body signs that he or she uses and that of others. The body comprises of various organs that work in synchrony in order to achieve symbiosis. When communicating using body language, there are various bodily organs that take part in this process. The various organs include:

Eyes

The eyes have time and again as the gate-path to your soul. This is because they tend to reveal the kind of person you are just by a single glimpse of the eyes. For instance, when an individual communicating to you, take note of how his or her eyes behave. For instance, are they keeping an eye to eye connection? When an individual is keeping an eye to eye contact, this is a pointer that they are keenly listening to you and paying attention. The eyes will tell a lot. When you want to know if someone is not listening to you, you just see that the individual is not maintaining eye contact whatsoever. The eyes can also be a source of intimidation. When accompanied by other gestures, the eye can be very revealing.

When a person is looking away during a conversation, this is a red light. The person may be either avoiding you or is too involved with other issues that what you are telling them will not sink. Some people do this as a cover-up of their feelings since they may be afraid of exposing them. In the Traditional African Society, looking down while someone is communicating was a sign of respect. It was exhibited mostly to the royals or to an elder. When the eyes are constantly blinking, this should be a pointer that there is a lot that the individual is thinking about. Often this individual may be restless. As earlier discussed, when an individual opens his or her eyes wide, this is as a result of being aroused by something or someone. It can also mean that the individual is interested or concentrating keenly on something.

Movements of the Head

These have been the most common body movements since time immemorial. For instance, a nod in the head will be a sign that somebody is saying yes. On the other hand, when the head shakes, this can be a denotation of saying no. Whereas this has been established, you need to be extra keen when checking on the head movements of a person. This is because an individual might express his or her affirmation about something while in the real sense they are shaking their head. This indicates that the person is not in acceptance of what he or she is saying.

Take an instance when you are talking to someone about something and their response is a slow nod. The person is saying yes and is encouraging you to continue talking because he is listening attentively. The opposite of this is when you are passing your idea to someone and the response in a quick nod. This means that there is a lot of irrelevancy in what you are trying to put across and that you should do away with it expeditiously. When the head pulls back and is in a rest position, this might be an indication that you are communicating something which he does not believe in its veracity.

Gestures

These refer to the direct signals that we make with our hands when we are communicating verbally. They work best in correlation. They can also be used in the singular. Take for instance when you lift your hand up, automatically people will understand that you have to put across and what you need to be given the floor. There are various hand gestures that do not require to be accompanied by any verbal justification. For instance, a thumb is a direct meaning of a go-ahead whereas a thumbs down would be used to denote rejection or inconsistency. There are various gestures however that vary in meaning from one place to another. There are also other gestures that denote two or more meanings that are different contextually.

Take for instance a thumbs up that are friendly in nature in the US and is used to denote a go-ahead carries an offensive meaning in the middle east countries. The first bump might be a form of greeting in the US whereas elsewhere it is a sign of freedom or liberation.

The body consists of various body parts that send messages. It is not only limited to hand gestures, face, and eyes as a means of communication. It formulates its own channels in the worst of scenarios. Our body posture, feet and how we position ourselves when communicating also tells a lot.

Chapter 6: Understanding Personality Types

There has been a heated debate on the subject of personality types. While some have adopted the view that there is no specific cluster to personality and that it is something that exists in a continuous for, others have attempted to classify personality types in accordance with a particular threshold. Research has it that there are a number of traits that can be used when attempting to deduce what type of personality is associated with that person. There exist five traits than can be employed when trying to find out what type of personality is a person.

The traits include extraversion, contentiousness, neuroticism, openness, and agreeableness. Once you have a clear comprehension of these traits, you are able to deduce where an individual is likely to fall in the hierarchy. These traits cut across to the extent that you are able to deduce the likeliness of someone contracting a particular disease by simply focusing on the traits.

Personality Traits

Openness

From the face value of it, openness can be used to refer to an encounter where there is a lack of restriction.

When it comes to a personality trait, openness may be used to refer to an individual who lacks concealment. This is a transparent individual who is often frank. This particular trait is used to show how open-minded a person can be. These types of people are often free-spirited in that they will engage in any novel idea that comes up. Their attributes do not stop at that but go further to encompass an imaginative attribute and one that is curios. When you are open-minded, you do not believe in the limits. You are always akin to break the limits and go higher. You have an inborn thought that you are able to conquer any limit. The opposite of open-minded is close-minded. Close-minded type of people are often satisfied with what they get and do not involve themselves in the business of trying new things.

Open-minded people will be keen to understand the most non-interesting topics that others would have shoved away. They have lots of ideas but this is often engraved in the emotional quotient. They do less in practical but they are the ones who come up with various ideas that can be put to practice. Most of these people are very creative. They are socially apt since they are able to communicate their ideas candidly. Openness can be broken down into various facets which include: artistic interests, liberty, imaginative, intellectual aptness, adventurous. Most jobs nowadays require people who have this type of personality. In order to fit in the job industry, you need to be an individual who is open to change, one who thinks critically and thinks on his or her feet. People who lack this kind of trait have an effect of doing well in jobs that are routine-based and not based on improving the model of a particular thing.

Neuroticism

From the wording of it, neurotic persons are those that have a neutral type of behavior. These are people who when faced with the normal factors of life they respond neutrally. These are the type of people who can be referred to as normal people facing anxiety issues. These types of people face a kind of disorder that is referred to as neurosis. Neurosis is a type of disorder that tends to distort the quality of life that an individual is leading without necessarily changing any facts about reality. Neurosis is a word that has been used to refer to the behavior of anxiety that an individual exhibits.

Neuroticism is a condition that exhibits a tendency of one being always on the negative or in a state of emotional anxiety. Neurosis sits far from this type of condition. People in this particular umbrella tend to suffer a great deal from the feeling of depression. The feeling of anxiety, guilt, anger, and envy often has a lasting effect. Sometimes its severity varies from one person to another. They are hurt by the environment in which they are in. To them, the environment brings more stress. The visualize getting through the day as a major setback. Every encounter in their lives is often agonizing. To some people, a problem comes, a solution is sought for and immediately the problem is disposed of. When it comes to these individuals, when a problem arises, they see it as the end of the world since they do not buy a point of view of seeking to remedy the problem but rather enhancing its personal effects. Often the meaning of neuroticism has been confused to men either psychosis or neurosis. It is key that one should understand the clear meaning of this trait in order to maintain consistency.

Agreeableness

From the wording of it, an agreeable person is one who goes with almost anything. These are the type of people who are friendly their and welcoming. It becomes subtle to quarrel with such kinds of people because they are attributed to have a warm heart view of the world is one that is optimal. These types of people tend to shove their interests in a bid to accommodate those of others. The opposite kind of these people is self-centered people who put their interests before others. These are the people you are likely to quarrel with due to their degree of not being cooperative. Individuals with this kind of trait are usually keen to foster a sense of well-being and harmony. They see as an important aspect to get in touch with others. This feeling is brought about by the tendency to agree on what the other party is talking about. When you are encountered with a problem, these are the type of individuals who will always be ready to help in any way. It is by nature that such kind of individuals is natural helpers. They have a very unique perception of the world that allows them to see the world from a very different perspective. Their belief is that the world is full of people who are morally apt.

Agreeableness is made up of some facets which include: sympathy, altruism, modesty, morality, trust, and cooperation. Agreeable people with the tendency of making a new friend and having an optimistic view of the world are often inclined to be good at team building, and pulling of masses together. In respect to career choices, an agreeable person is not likely to fit in any career specifically. Research has it that most of these people who are not good at agreeing with others form a great basis for critics and people who look for mistakes where there is none.

Extroversion

This particular type of person has a tendency to be outgoing. Socially they are apt people who tend to interact with anyone. They find joy in spending time with people and taking part in various activities that involve a number of people. They lead lives that are full of energy and happiness. The opposite of extraversion is introversion. These are the types of people who find joy in being alone. Most of the time they seclude themselves from gatherings and stay alone. Introverts live a very lonely life. Extroverts find joy when mingling with the rest of the World. They have a liking of being in groups that tend to seek attention from the outside world. They engage in various activities in order to stay in the light. This kind of person leads a very vibrant life one that is full of locomotion.

Extroversion comes with a number of traits that are not limited to cheerfulness, assertiveness, gregariousness, friendliness, and excitement seeking and activity level. When it comes to the job market, the levels of extroversions will vary. There is one that will be useful to high extroverts who wish to interact with people time and again. If you are working alone, lower levels of extroversion will be required.

Conscientiousness

This is a trait that is associated with being extra careful in whatever you indulge in. These types of people carry out their duties diligently and are keen to ensure that what they do is in perfect state. These are people who are not prone to shortcuts. If it is in the employment field, they work there any to the top of the food chain without engaging shortcuts. They are well-organized people since they plan for something before it actually happens. This shows how keen and serious they are. Research has it that people with a high level of conscience are always inclined to perform better in school as compared to those with lower levels. These people view challenges as stepping blocks towards greater heights. They encounter a problem with open arms, own it and take responsibility. With this kind of approach, they are more likely to find solutions to their problems rather than encountering a problem and letting it eat you from within. These types of individuals experience longer lives because they are very observant of what they take into their bodies. Often this does not relate to lesser drinking and smoking only but it also cuts across various factors that contribute to a longer and healthier life.

Research has it that people who exhibit this kind of trait are generally successful in life. The lives of these kinds of people tend to become successful owing to the super-organization. As we all know failing to plan is like planning to fail. These individuals have this saying at the back of their minds all their lives.

Personality types

Research that was focused on the study of human beings had the following findings. The research was to the effect that most of our population can be put into four clusters of classification depends on personality traits. It was found that there are four personality traits that vary from individual to individual. They are: Pessimistic, optimistic, trusting and envious.

Pessimistic Personality

In order to fully comprehend what a pessimistic personality entails, we need to appreciate the meaning of a pessimist. This is an individual whose state of mind is inclined to think of the worst outcomes possible. A pessimist is a person who expresses no hope that an outcome will take a particular direction. Normally people tend to attribute pessimism as being rooted in an event that took place in the past. This event may be recurrent in nature. This may not be the case as this particular type of individual have a fixed belief system that makes them take a particular type of direction which is pessimism. In order for one to appreciate his or her condition as a pessimist, there are a number of factors that need to appear. These are normally the pointers towards knowing if a person is a pessimist or not. They include but are not limited to:

You are obliged to visualize things in a negated manner. For instance, one individual may see a half-empty glass whereas the other individual may visualize a half-full glass. The discrepancy that lays between these two individuals is often that one is attracted to the negative part of a subject whereas the other is attracted to the opposite side of the subject. People with pessimistic personality types are often drawn towards the negative side of issues. With this negative attitude in place, the worst of occurrences to them becomes normality. In this sense, they tend to embrace the fact that the outcome will often have two implications. Either a win or a loose. Learning to embrace the loose is what makes these people move on from previous worst circumstances.

These people are often realists because their personality is premised on the fact that there are times when you can gather a win or a loss in life. What makes us bolder is how we respond to the loss. These people are not the actual "prophets of doom" but rather they take the hat of analysts. This because they evaluate every possible outcome and then they learn to sit with the worst of outcomes. Owing to this, it will be safe to deduce that these people are always ready to take up any feedback. With the experience of always landing in a bad encounter, these people have no meaning for the word forgiveness. They often buy the school of thought that if an individual has done it once, most likely the event will re-occur. When visualizing the worst of outcomes, you are often inclined to prevent it before it happens. Take for instance you are on a bridge and you see children playing by the rails. You might take up to yourself to remove them from the rails because your vision is that they may end up falling into the river. Pessimists tend to go deeper into issues in order to evaluate various outcomes. Their effect on inter-personal relationships is that you may never be able to trust someone again.

When you encounter pessimists, you should avoid engaging in deep verbal brawls with them. You should make sure that you do not attach yourself to their negativity because it can eat you up in ways you have no experience. Keep a positive attitude and pay less attention to what they are saying.

Optimistic Personality

Optimisms in relation to personality. An optimistic person is an individual who has the best interests at heart. These types of people usually focus on the best things in life. They have a focus that makes them buy from the school of thought that everything will be okay. Optimistic people see the negative side of life and accept it. They are always in search of the brighter side of life since the dark side is not favorable. These types of people have an open heart. They tend to accept everyone even those who might have been rejected elsewhere. These people are connected to things that will always heighten their overall emotions. When your emotions tend to be heightened all the time, research has it that you live a better and healthier life that is devoid of a certain stress. This is because you are able to manage stress as soon as it erupts. People with this kind of trait tend to exhibit compassion. This is because they care about the well-being of others. They extend this compassion to non-living thins which may include nature. When we show other people that we have some degree of caring for them, in turn they will return the favor. This is what enhances positive living. These individuals gratitude on their way. They are always thankful even to the simplest of things. For instance, you might be stressing that your house needs some renovations or perhaps you need to move out and relocate. To these people they will be grateful that they even have a roof over their heads. With a positive mindset, these individuals will always be inclined to think that things will turn for the better. They are forgiving in nature and do not hold grudges whatsoever. They act as inspiration to others due to the lives they lead. They are always smiling and this is what lights up their mood. The look at every perspective in a manner that is positive and they are always keen to be grateful when it goes their way.

These kinds of people are generally good. You will often be inclined to be around them. This is because they are always positive and will elevate your mood whenever you think that you have fallen low below the bedrock.

Envious Personality

Envy relates to the feeling that you are the one who deserved the better position that the adverse party may be in. Envious people have a tendency of looking down upon others. Envious people are often not trustworthy. This is because they do not want you to actually know of their progress in life. They will always express a feeling of anger towards you when your projects go through. This is because they thrive when your projects do not. They are happy when you are suffering or in pain. Competition is what defines their lives and most of the time you will find that they pick up on anyone without any particular reason. They are the biggest judges since they tend to follow up on your life, what you do and after that decide for you whether what you are doing is good or bad in their eyes. When they see you making friends, they are keen to make sure that this kind of relationship does not last.

When you encounter such people, you should be keen enough to not talk to them much about your plans and strategies. In short, leave them the way you found them. In order to avoid these kinds of people, one should consider making friends with people who are in the same economic class as you. In order to find out whether that person talks about you, you should consider finding out from a mutual friend whether this is the case.

Trusting Personality

Generally, agreeable individuals will fall under this bracket. These types of people are the ones who will believe in you at first instance without suspecting any ill motives. They are outgoing in nature. An individual with whom you rust will always exhibit integrity. Integrity is the act of doing what you are supposed to do when you are supposed to do it. They exhibit high levels of honesty because they are trustworthy. Owing to this fact, you can say that these particular individuals are dependable. They are consistent in whatever they say because the truth shall always come to light. These people are transparent to the extent that they cannot lie on a particular fact in order to misrepresent you. Most of them carry with them the best of intentions.

Many times, these people have faced betrayal since they trust anyone without question. This type of betrayal often ends them in losses. However, these type of people have time and again proven to be the best companions.

Chapter 7: The Use of NLP in Dark Psychology

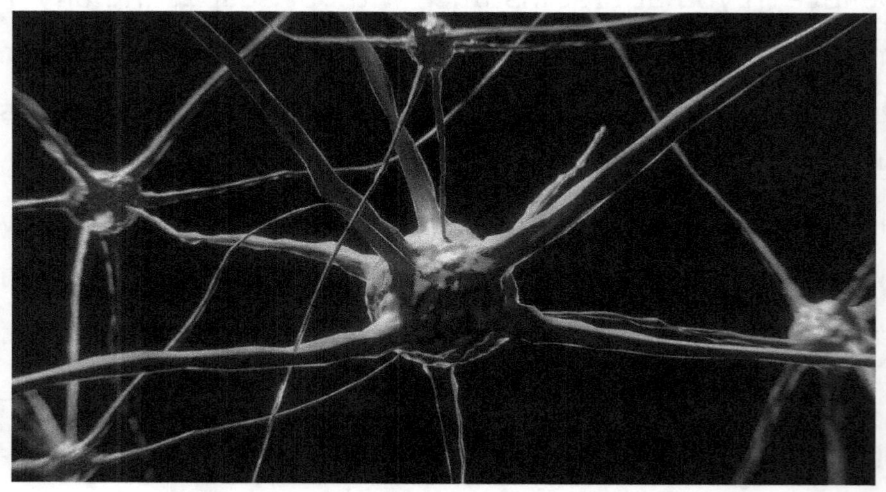

NLP has already been defined in the earlier chapters of this book. NLP is a type of language that is used for the brain or to extract information from it. This brings us close to the topic at hand which is dark psychology. As you have read the topics that came ahead you saw that dark psychology is all about our relation to our minds and others too. We have seen the types of dark psychology people use on use. We have seen how similar and different they all are. They all play their role in the circle of dark psychology. So how does NLP and dark psychology work hand in hand since both have a relation to the mind? It is very simple since one is the language and the other is the means. That simply puts how they both work together. The NLP is like the guide to how dark psychology works on people. One should understand how to read others before being able to understand how they will use dark psychology on other people. This is the importance of knowing the interrelation between these two very important aspects of life. So how does NLP extract information from the mind?

There are five ways in which NLP extracts information from the mind of someone. The first is known as the named entry recognition. This is one of the most powerful techniques that is used in NLP. This is based on picking information from the names. That could be your name, address, company, and phone number. This may be picked out of a system call from someone. This is the basic way to know about someone since that is the most basic information that they have in their lives. As the name suggests the name entry one is able to fill in the gaps about someone. With this information, one can find out a lot about someone just because of the basics. Basics lead obviously to the complex matter. With this type of information extract technique, it follows the grammar rules and the information is organized. This way the information can easily be retrieved if there is a need for that. These are the basic points of this technique I have covered. There is obviously more to it but these are what you should know about the name entry recognition technique.

The other is known as sentiment analysis. This is actually the most commonly used technique NLP. It is mostly used in surveys. In the most common cases, the results are taken as positive, negative or neutral. This is for the normal cases what about where this is not a normal case? The numbers are basically put or recorded in their numerical form but in more than the usual category. From the name we get sentiment analysis we get the sentiment. This means that the times of the analysis are so many thus this type of information gathering may be a little useless if one needs stable information. That is why most surveys have three choices in them thus helping to separate the positive numbers from the negative and the neutral. This then helps someone to know where the issue is and where a good job has been done. It is also used in activities like forest checking or even in marine checking. This is to know how these natural resources are doing. Thus, this method is very popular since it is used almost everywhere and in every aspect of our lives. This is another technique to note very keenly.

Text summarization is another technique used in NLP. As the name suggests it works with summarizing ideas or text. This is mostly done in articles or texts. This is where you just take the text that seems important and that is what you use. This is mostly done by companies when they are advertising themselves. They ask themselves. What would captivate the reader? What will make the reader be interested in reading what we are advertising? The point is that the information should be keyed in from the interests that exist to the reader. One should not just dump everything in. it works hand in hand with sentiment analysis. It helps to pick the right statement to use in articles. This is mostly done in a system to determine the perfect fit. Then the article or newspaper can be written. This technique majorly deals with seeing how humans think and react to a certain aspect. It reads what the human mind wants to see and wants to be brought to their attention. This is how the media industry catches attention all the time since they already know what we want from them. They know we want what is important and juicy.

Also, there is aspect mining. It works with sentiment analysis too. This happens during text summarization where the content of a message has to be picked. Aspect mining looks into the aspect part of the information while the sentiment part analyzes the whole text to see what will be taken positive, negative or even neutral by the public in general. These two techniques are what make text summarization possible. They also determine the take of the public to a certain issue that will or has been brought to life. With this technique, one has the feel will to extract any information they please to. In this technique, the text, the input, and the output are all looked into. They matter to the subject that is being discussed. Chances are not left to the unknown. Everything is scrutinized before it is released. Every calculation is made to see the outcome that will follow the release. This technique shows when to stop, what to take up and what to leave. Everything that the people will think once the article or message is released. Their opinions really matter in these techniques and that is why it is there to make the remarks positive and acceptable.

The final technique is topic modeling. This finally takes up after the use of sentiment analysis and aspect mining. It is there to fix the text summarization. After finding out what the people want and what they do not some rehabilitation is what takes place. What is this rehabilitation I speak of? This is where you make something new and try and use all the techniques that have been offered to you. They help to give you a clear path on which you can take to rehabilitation. This is the most important point to take in. The topic modeling is just brought all the corrections done before together to make something into something bigger and better. So, what are the aspects that topic modeling uses? It has a few ways in which it is used to make it effective for the general public who will get the information. First, there is the latent semantic analysis which comes from sentiment analysis. Probabilistic latent semantic analysis is also another example. Another is latent Dirichlet allocation and finally, there is the correlated topic model.

These are all the aspects that help in making topic modeling success in the field of NLP and all it contains.

NLP is an easy way to read one's mind. In short, it helps dark psychology. Dark psychology as stated before deals with persuasion, deception, manipulation, narcissism and even psychopaths. All this information should help you figure out how they work together. For someone skilled in the art of NLP reading others is no hustle. All they have to do is look at you and your behaviors. That is all that it takes for them to find out a lot about you. This may be following body movements, eye contact, listening to the way you speak and even following on your behaviors. With these small observations one may come up with all of these: one may find out the side of the brain in which you really use a lot. Another thing is that they will find the sense you tend to use a lot in your daily activities. Also, he or she will find out what part of your brain you use to store all the information you take in. Finally, he or she will find out where you make up all your information from. Of course, which side of the brain you use to do that is what I mean.

So how is NLP used in Dark Psychology?

The first is through hypnosis. Hypnosis is a technique that is used by psychologists or psychiatrists. It helps them to retrieve the hidden things in the unconscious minds of their patients. It is one of the psychoanalysis techniques that exist. They help you dig in the hidden past and answer some questions that were unclear to you. It is like the doorway to the buried issues in the unconscious. Most of what is trying to be uncovered is usually from one's past that their mind probably wants it hidden or it was a coping mechanism. Hypnosis is being able to read the unconscious mind. Find all the aspects that have been hidden from us. Finding out the reason why these memories are hidden away in a place where reaching it is not so easy. This is where NLP comes in and it makes hypnosis easy. It is a program used in mind reading. So, it helps the psychiatrist to see what your unconscious mind holds and what the best way of retrieving the hidden information is. To understand all these you must first understand the conscious and the pre-conscious mind.

The other way it helps is in finding deceptive people. Deception is the art of giving half-truths. This is basically like lying but only halfway. This means that these people give you what you want to hear and the less of what you do not want to hear. Over the years people have come up with contraptions that are used to detecting a lie. These contraptions include: polygraph machines, lie detector machines and recently they have found a way of making truth serums. All these have been made to catch deceivers and not leaving the liars out of this. These have been used especially by the authorities during the investigation of crimes. So how do these contraptions or scientific research work? How are they involved with NLP? The answer is simple. NLP is the main ingredient of how the work. First, you must understand the person then find out how they operate. The contraptions have also been made in a way that when you are connected to them then understand you will be easy. You are asked questions and when you lie or tell the truth halfway they will just find you. This method is easy since the machine does the work for the human.

NLP is also used in brainwashing. What is brainwashing? Brainwashing is the act reprogramming one's brain. It is where one can be changed their ideas and mindset and a new you given to you. The new you will have a new way of thinking, new ideas and also new perspectives to life. The person who reprograms you makes you into their minion or puppet. You follow all that he or she says to you. It is like you are a min him or her. Your thoughts and actions are what they want you to do. This is possible for someone who can hack your mind. Only a person with the knowledge of NLP can do that. The study you and know who you really are. That is from behavior to how you think and whole who and what you are. This is where they know how to start manipulating you and leading you into their ways. They know your strengths and weaknesses. They know all your blind spots in which they can use against you and so in the very end they have you in their grasp. All you do is in their bidding.

Another way is by playing mind games. In mind games, one finds the thing that makes you feel vulnerable. That means to find your weak or blind spot. With this knowledge, they know how to play with you. Find what makes you vulnerable is easy. You just have to study the person. Get close to them so that it is easy to study them. Study their behavior and way of communication. Get to know their thinking patterns. Know how they react to different issues that arise in their daily living. Know their emotions and whether they show them in front of others. These are the secrets to mind games. NLP people are diverse in such doing so for them to make mind games happen is so easy they make it seem like taking water. For them studying someone could take only a few days and with that, they can be able to play with your mind without a care in the world. To them this seems like a harmless toy to play with. They do not realize the damage to them it's all fun and games on their part. This is how NLP makes mind games a big success in terms of dark psychology.

Also, NLP helps narcissistic people. These are people who only care about themselves. What matters is their lives and what's in them. They use others to get to the top. As they use them at the very end they let go of them since they are a one-person ride. They have so many techniques that they use on others like smear campaigns. They know when they need you and when they do not. They also know how to keep you around them. They know what you deeply desire and what they do is give it to you when they need you then they take it away when they are done with you. It is usually hard for the victim to give them up since they have that effect. Where then does NLP come in? it comes to the point where they are looking for their stepping stone that means that the person they use then throw away. They know who can be manipulated and who cannot and so they use that to their advantage. They get to know what you desire and with that, they draw you to their side and make you stay there until otherwise.

The other is persuasion. Some people think that this is harmless but it is not. It is not just doing bidding for someone just once. Some people say it was just once. These persuasive people can make doing again if they see that you were up to it once. What they do is to whisper to your ear and tell you should do something. They convince you with sweet words and reasons why you should do it. They make you into a puppet even if it is in that moment that you do their bidding. You become somewhat like their servant for that period of time. So, what makes NLP successful in the art of persuasion? These people find what you really want and a reason that would make do the deed that they need you to do. So, the point is looking for your weakness and somehow made into a way to convince. They know you and they use that against you. This is mainly used by people who really know you like, friends, family, workmates, and even classmates. This is one method that people assume and thinking that is no cause of alarm in any way.

The second last is psychopathy. This is the act in which psychopaths do. Psychopaths are believed to be dangerous to the people. They cannot live in society since they are dangerous to themselves and others. They normally look for a target and they look for a way to attack them. They normally attack in all forms. That means physically, mentally and even psychologically. They choose someone depending on their like or based on something they went through. They like stocking and being in the shadows which is very creepy and very unusual for most of the normal people. They can kill and do not find that very hard to do. They are also very unstable emotionally. They can act up at any time without notice. NLP is what they choose their victims with. They may look for the most vulnerable people or for those who seem like they own the world as revenge. They easily get obsessed with someone and if they do their actions are unpredictable hence can hurt anyone in their way. These people are very dangerous and should seek professional help from other psychiatrists. They are unfit to live in society just like that with no help.

Finally, there is Machiavellianism. This is where someone uses cunning methods to get what he or she wants. One can do so many things to get what they want in this type of condition. The only thing that matters is what they want and by hook or crook, they must get it. They forget to use the right means and they always will choose to use the crooked means in their lives. So, what is important to them is their goals. They are manipulative hence they know how to apply NLP in their lives for their goals to come to form. So, in all these, we have seen the works of NLP and how they work everywhere round to make dark psychology possible and a success. They both deal with the mind and how it works. They are both bound together. There is no dark psychology without NLP around. It is important to know how dark psychology comes about from NLP. There is so much that I have not dealt with in the uses of NLP in dark psychology but the given information should shed some light on the topic. This was important to know if you are to understand dark psychology. These are the ideas to grasp in your mind in terms of dark psychology in relation to NLP.

Chapter 8: The power of emotional manipulation

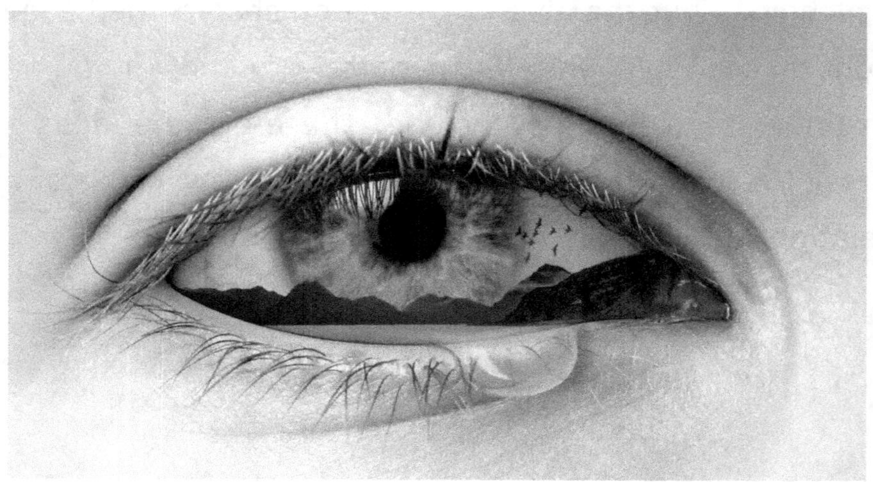

Emotional manipulation is the behavior that is supposed to change the stance of other people through deceptive and to some extent, abusive ways. It is also known as psychological manipulation, advanced empathy, emotion control, induced empathy or pathogenesis.

Types of Emotional Manipulators

There are different types of emotional manipulators, but today we will only expound on 10 of them. It is good to note that they are not limited to the ten that are in this article.

The Victim

I am sure that we have all met the victim in our lives at one time. They are always complaining and are insecure about one thing or more about their experiences. They will always push for your approval and pity. They will make you feel sorry for them and at the same time, give you the power to uplift their spirits and make them feel better. Regardless of what has happened, the victim turns and twists the situation to become the victim. The victim turns people against each other and gains power and control. They mostly struggle with anger and fear issues, and some even become paranoid. They are always on the receiving end, not being liked, are ever betrayed, nobody cares about them, etc.

The Expert or One-Up-Manship

These have a strong need to be better than everyone else, and they have mastered the art that you cannot notice their insecurities. They will always compare themselves to you and try to belittle you at every chance they get. They never miss an opportunity to say it in your face or through their actions how they are better than you. They have a toxic personality and will continuously point out every little mistake you make. They are a dangerous kind and will always make you full of their insecurities. This kind will know all your weak points and never hesitate to use them to manipulate you and not make you feel better.

The Self-Defender

A normal human being will always seek to apologize when they make a mistake. The self-defender emotional manipulators are never on the wrong; they always blame everyone but themselves. They will always guilt trip you and make you feel bad for everything that goes a miss. This kind never takes the blame for any offense they make.

The Flirty Type

We all know someone or even better some of us have a friend who is always flirty. They never have boundaries and will easily flirt with your ex or current partner. The always give more of themselves to others and always seem desperate to do so. They are so toxic and will forever destroy any good thing in your life, be it a job or a relationship and make you feel bad for it. Most of them use sex as a tool to gain power and attention. They will easily break a relationship or even marriage and happily gloat about it. They feel empowered when they watch systems fall.

The Intimidator

The intimidator bullies his way around with words like, "You don't want to see me angry" or "If you dare do that, I will mess you up". They are very demanding and always insist that you have to do what they want. The ones who are physically huge use their physique and even adapt a threatening posture to intimidate their victims. They take their victims as pawns that can be bent and moved anytime to get what they want. If you dare oppose them or refuse their demands, they will force you and use aggression to make you give in.

The Blasters (The Outbursts of Anger)

"How can you do that? Are you stupid? It is your entire fault."

The blasters use anger outbursts to avoid issues at hand that need your attention. They have anger management issues and are never angry with you but themselves. They are angry at themselves for some unknown reasons only known to them and always project them by being mad at you. They never take responsibility for their actions and to avoid being questioned; they scream, make threats or yell at you. An excellent example in a relationship is the blaster will blame you for his infidelity and claim it's your fault you were not there.

The Innocent Liar or Intentional Miss-Interpreter

The innocent liar is a dangerous type that will make up a story to sound fascinating. You should be careful with this kind as they are desperate to be liked. They tell lies about their victims and purposely interpreting wrongly what their victims say. They may seem to be friendly and outgoing to have the upper hand and gain personal information from you. When discovered and confronted, they will act all teary and back down. They tell innocent lies, but you should be very careful as you won't also know whether they are telling the truth on trivial matters.

The Victorious Weakling or the Powerful Dependents

They disguise themselves as being weak but gain power over their victims. They stroke their victim's ego and depend on them. They will act weak and allow you to gain a sense of control to rely on you. If you resist their dependency, they stop being nice and become real nasty quickly. They are self-centered and aim at gaining their needs regardless of the pain caused by others.

Triangle or Divider Who Conquers

The triangle is famously known to seek approval and love from all the people that surround them. They use that advantage to understand the current information and use it to gossip. They act nice and play all innocent to gain your trust. They use lies and distortions to manipulate people. After obtaining your trust and private information from you, they will distort it and spread rumors about you. They will ally with other people to gain power and control over their victims. They are single-minded and want to hurt people emotionally. Anger fuels them. They make good leaders as their followers are people with low self-esteem.

The Projector

We have all heard of the saying that a pot calling the kettle black, there is no better saying to describe them. The projector will never take responsibility for their actions, and when questioned they become defensive. They always blame others for their flaws and behaviors. Unlike a triangle that recruits people to their corner to prey on their victim, the projector recruits them to avoid accountability. Their intentions are never to hurt others. If they don't get what they want from you, they will bad mouth and trash you. They always project their evil characters on their victims. Blame-game is their secret card, and they use it to justify their awful behaviors.

For all the above emotional manipulators to succeed, they prey on the victim's weak points. It is a smart move, and they mostly manage to use it.

Characteristics and Signs of Emotional Manipulators

In this context, we will look at the attributes of emotional manipulators. If we all knew their characteristics, we could easily escape their traps. Without further ado, here are some common qualities of emotional manipulators.

- Secrecy- They are secretive and work behind the scenes to achieve their goals. Sometimes they brag after their success on preying on you.
- They are good listeners and pay attention to details. They quickly pick points from your conversations to start controlling you.
- They are deceptive.
- They have a domineering personality.
- Their ideology precedes yours at all times.
- They have no boundaries and have little or no regard for who they hurt along the way.
- They let you speak first.
- They twist facts.
- They make you feel sorry for airing your concerns.

- When they say something mean or rude, they are always, "just kidding".
- They always criticize you.
- They use your fears and insecurities against you.
- In times of crisis, they are always "too calm".
- Their actions and words don't match.
- They are experts at leveraging your guilt.
- They perfect the role of the victim.
- They are always eager to help then later act like a martyr.
- They know all your weak-spots and use that information against you.
- They always have worse problems than you.
- They are an emotional black hole and suck everyone to those emotions.
- They skip a few steps in any relationship and expect the same from you.
- They are skilled liars and undermine your grasp of reality.

Emotional Manipulation Techniques

So, after knowing the different types of emotional manipulators and their characteristics, what are the techniques that they apply to manipulate you? We will discuss some of their tactics, but we should note that they are not limited to these only. Each day the manipulators come up with better techniques to gain control over their victims. Without wasting time, let's dive into the most commonly used techniques by emotional manipulators.

Projection

In this tactic, the manipulator shifts their weakness to someone else. They never take responsibility for their actions and instead blame it on another person. They always paint themselves clean and make the other person look dirty. When there is a problem, they always find a victim to blame. People who easily notice faults in others project their negative selves. A proud person will easily notice the pride in others. In the projection technique, the manipulator will always seek to make others look weak while they come out as strong.

Gaslighting

To gaslight is to make someone have doubts about their character or action about themselves that is real. Emotional manipulators are fond of this tactic. They use questions to doubt something factual. In case of a success story, they will make you feel like it was just a dream. An excellent example in a relationship is when you suspect that there is infidelity or an affair, and instead of getting answers, you are bombarded with questions that will make you think that it is only your imagination. Gaslighting is one reason why most people are stuck in unhealthy relationships. To get rid of this emotional manipulation, experts advice victims to document events and happenings and frequently go through it so that a manipulator cannot go to the extent of even making them doubt their existence.

Denial

Lying, distortion of facts and denial are in the DNA of an emotional manipulator. A manipulator will agree with some truths to use it to control you later. They intentionally agree with the truth and then deny it. They change the rules when the game is still on and leave the victim confused. The victim is left blaming himself with no knowledge that he is dealing with an emotional manipulator. They are a dangerous type and are always a step ahead in planning their game. They always foresee the outcome and plan on denying ever being involved in the game.

Intimidation

In intimidation, the manipulator identifies your weak points like fear and capitalizes on them. They intimidate their victims to silence. Once they realize that you are easily scared or frightened, they use threats or strange body language to instill fear in you, and you lose your trail of thoughts and end the argument or discussion. Where possible, you should avoid showing your fears to people you can't trust.

Intellectual Bullying

The manipulator uses mental facts to overwhelm you. They may be wrong, but they know that there is no way to prove that. It is not possible to know everything, but we should strive to have a little knowledge of everything. Knowledge will come in hand in case of intellectual bullying, you will not be swept off your feet with information, and you can easily predict the validity of the information or not. This kind of manipulation is famous for financial institutions. The only remedy for this manipulation is always to strive to be informed.

Intentional Digression

Digression is differing from the ordinary course of a conversation to something completely unrelated to the topic at hand. When a manipulator makes a mistake and does not want to be held accountable for the act, he digresses to another issue, preferably one of your favorites. He already knows your weakness and manipulates you to overlook his mistake. In such a situation, only prior knowledge of emotional techniques can come in hand and save you from falling for their tricks.

Name Calling

Emotional manipulators have a very high opinion of themselves but a false one. They are narcissists and are always right when everyone else is on the wrong. When you question their idea or thoughts and bruise their ego, they result in name-calling. They are not ashamed and can utter any obscene word on earth to put you down. People who have not developed a tough skin will easily succumb to this technique. They are silenced and denied to air their opinion. It is not fun having someone calling you names and to some extent in the presence of a crowd and worse still his fanatics. The only way to handle this is to have a thick skin and unflinchingly inform the manipulator that you will not accept any name-calling.

Conditioning

Conditioning is a technique of training a person to act in a specific manner as wanted by the trainer. In emotional manipulation, the manipulator does this secretly, and the victim will not realize when being cornered. The victim gets rid of their ideas or values and gradually embraces those of the manipulator. Do you think conditioning can make a good human being out of the previous scrupulous one? Does the technique work for good, or is it only for turning good to bad? No, if it for a good cause, it is a healthy social influence, and it is always a give and take situation. In manipulation, one person is manipulated for the benefit of the other and one's selfish reasons.

Stalking and Gossiping

Every emotional manipulation aims at controlling you. When managing you becomes difficult, the manipulator easily camouflages and control how people view you. In this case, emotional manipulation is achieved by gossiping and spreading lies about you. They spread lies and rumors about you to your peers and other people. They give people wrong intuition about you. Some even go to the extent of even stalking and monitoring you.

A good example is when you are in a relationship with such kind of a person, and you are at the verge of breaking up because of their bad habits they take advantage of that and gossip you to others so they may view you in the wrong. In such a case, people never get to know the truth but in the end blame and see you on a bad angle. Everyone will view you as a bad person who broke their trust whereas you are the victim.

Bad Surprises

Surprises are pleasant, especially coming from our loved ones. On the other hand, to an emotional manipulator, surprises are tools to catch you unawares and throw you off guard. An emotional manipulator will agree to keep a promise and then at the eleventh hour say it won't be possible. That is what we call a bad surprise as you had already let your guard down and at this point, they bring out their demands. They always employ their tactics in a tricky manner, and you will never know how they hit you.

Emotional manipulation is a selfish adventure, and we can only avoid such by educating ourselves on their tactics so as not fall victim. We can also educate ourselves on the signs to look out for to know if you are emotionally manipulated.

Signs of Emotional Manipulation

How can you tell that you are under emotional manipulation? These signs are not easy to spot as the manipulator is someone we trust, and we want to believe they have our best interests at heart. With that said, if there is any doubt or hint of emotional manipulation, these are the signs we should look for.

You Have Feelings of Fear, Obligation, and Guilt

When a victim is being manipulated, he is coerced to do something they want to do. The victim feels fear to do it or obligated to do it, and when he thinks of not doing it, he feels guilty for that. The bully uses fear and threats to control their target while the victim makes them feel guilty. The victim always acts hurt while in reality, they are the ones who caused the problem.

You Question Yourself Always

Gaslighting makes people question their memory, ideas, and reality. A manipulator twists what a victim says and makes it about him. There is a false sense of defensiveness or guilt if you are manipulated in that manner. You will feel as if you have done something wrong or failed while it's not the case. You should also note that the manipulator never takes responsibility but always blames.

There Are Strings Attached to Every Favor

Manipulators' favors are not just for fun and free. No, they are strings attached to it. This behavior is confusing as the victim never notices anything going wrong. With every good deed done, they are always an expectation. If the victim doesn't meet the expectations of a manipulator, he tags the victim as ungrateful.

You Observe the 'Foot-In-The-Door' and the 'Door-In-The-Face' Techniques

The foot-in-the-door techniques are whereby a person starts with a little and rational request that leads to a big request. This technique is common in street scams.

The door-in-the-face technique is the opposite where a person starts with a big request like a large sum of money and when you decline they ask for a smaller amount. The smaller appeal seems reasonable than, the bigger one and in this case you are bound to give in.

Chapter 9: Advanced Techniques to Develop a Powerful and Non-Manipulatable Mind

So, in this chapter, we are going to look at some of the techniques that will help you develop a healthy mind which will help read manipulation from afar and avoid it like a pro.

Know That There is More Than What is on the Surface

Being aware of your thoughts, beliefs, and state of being is a great way to start developing your mind into a powerful thing that someone cannot manipulate easily. But that is just a start. To be convincing enough, you will need to be aware of your subconscious mind.

Life events, especially those high impact ones, tend to leave us traumatized even after we believe that we have made a recovery. This trauma then means that we become a little paranoid and are likely to get emotional when we come across something visceral and profound.

When this happens, you become vulnerable to manipulation, with manipulators likely to then use your emotional state of being to talk you into something that benefits them and harms you.

Therefore, when you create awareness with your more profound thoughts and beliefs and emotions, you take away the power from the manipulator and become the one in control.

When the emotions in us begin to take control of us and take up space in our subconscious, then it reveals itself in the conscious through making us easy to be talked to into something we should not be doing.

If for example you have been heartbroken and do not have a sharp mind, it would be easy for someone new to come into your life and talk you into another relationship Or perhaps someone could come and tell you to do something that at that moment you are not in total control of due to the emotional breakdown. Like a case where after the death of their parents, a couple of siblings were talked into selling their parents primal land by a bunch of conmen who played on their broken emotional state, convincing the children that selling the property was something their parents would want.

Psychologists know that when we get a strong emotion within us, we get paralyzed, and will not think straight. This reaction is by design, according to Robert Dawson, Ph.D., a psychologist. Dawson states that this was meant to kick in our survival instinct, thus leading to an emotional reaction. So, being aware of your emotions will help you take more control of them, and you will then be able to hold on to your logic in the presence of a manipulator.

Be Aware of Your Sensitivity and How Someone May Use it Against You

We are all sensitive, some more than others. If a manipulator targets you, then they will often you and try to find your sensitive spots, your insecurities, things that bring dissatisfaction into you, things about you that you hid from the world. Then, they will move in and poke at it like someone poking at a fire with a stick, with the intent of causing an emotional reaction from you. Since you are sensitive about yourself, you will then fall into their traps, and they will be able to entice you into believing that they will provide you with relief, but this will often come at your loss.

A manipulator will often gain your trust before they strike. When they hit, they are so ruthless that they leave you viscerally damaged, more vulnerable yet again to more manipulations. When say you are someone shy and socially awkward and therefore very self-conscious, a master manipulator will study you and identify that you are anxious among people. Perhaps you seem eager to please. This person then moves in and begins to make small talks with you. You get excited. 'Someone saw me and came to talk to me!' But you are very conscious, so you stay put. They have studied you, so they know your vulnerabilities and keep at it. You begin to trust them. They offer you friendship, and in exchange, you give them your trust. You hang out together, visit each other, and even arrange camping. Then, before you know it, they hit you with a sucker punch. This is the technique that some serial killers like Alton Coleman used. They would take note of people and then use manipulation of what made them emotional to gain their trust then afterward, betray that trust by murdering them in cold blood.

It won't get that far with most manipulators though. But being aware of your sensitivities helps you build awareness of what people will use to manipulate you. Remember, people outside often will see this in you when you don't.

You can do this by looking back at events in the past and see what makes you vulnerable, what you want to keep hidden from the world. Look at what made you easy to manipulate in the past. What was the common mistake you made? What moves did the manipulator make that made you lower your guards? Are you easy to manipulate by people that you love? Do you feel like you are too trusting, too soon? Do people find it easy to make you guilty for their mistakes?

Or, if you trust your friends and family enough, ask them what makes you so sensitive. Then, write them down and begin being aware of them and how you react to them.

However, when you try to hide your vulnerability, it will still manifest in other ways that you are not conscious. As we have said, this is something that exists in a part of your mind that you have little control over. Besides, someone who is skilled at manipulation will often be able to tear off any mask because of their repeated dealing with cases of that respect.

Instead, acknowledge them and become aware of how they manifest.

Focus on What You Can Control

One of the ways that manipulators will often find their way with you will be through taking advantage of your weak mental state. How does this show?

Do you often find yourself always worried about things beyond your control? When you run into a problem, do you often see the actions that you need to take as not enough?

One of the main ways that people show weak mental strength is when they chose to focus on the more significant part of a problem that is beyond their control. When this happens, they get drained quickly of their mental energy and become emotionally vulnerable. For example, you get an engine failure out in the wild. Your phone is dead, or perhaps there is poor reception. What do you do? Do you stop the motorists passing by? What if they aren't to be trusted? So, instead of worrying about how to get the engine running, you begin to worry that the people passing might be out to harm you. So, you don't make an effort to stop passing cars. Time is moving. The night is approaching fast. Soon, you find yourself unable to do anything. When you get to this point, then it is ripe time for a manipulator to come in.

Knowing that you are desperate and have drained yourself of mental sharpness, they will then set about pressing the buttons that they know I'll get you to lower your guards, then, boom! They strike, and your worst fears become a self-fulfilling prophecy.

Falling into this feeling of helplessness and despair often comes with a sense of being unable to control your fortune. When you resign to fate, then fate won't take over in the way you want. Therefore, you will then relinquish your control to people out to harm you, or make a kill off of you.

Take charge of the situation. One way you can build this is through writing down instances where you have encountered a problem and how you reacted to that. Do you often take charge of what you can control? Or do you often feel helpless until somehow it goes away? If you had been manipulated before, what weaknesses did the other party exploit?

Then, you can begin to write through the actions that you will take in the event of trouble. I will get back to looking for a job when I fail this interview. I will take the time to heal after this heartbreak. I will...and so on. When you make yourself a proactive player in the script you are creating, you develop a strong mentality. You become a 'badass' and can channel this to the world, and in return, manipulators will steer clear. And if one is bold enough to try you, you will be able to identify them before they say and word and play along, turning them into the hunted.

Practice Making Yourself Tolerant to Your fears

What do you fear most? Rejection? Heartbreak? Is it vulnerability?

Look within you and try to find what makes you scared. When someone wants to manipulate you, these are the spots that they will want to target. Despite what we believe, when we are scared of something, then we become more available to come across it and fail spectacularly at spotting it.

When your biggest fear is rejection, then you will not make a move, thus, making it such that the rejection is automatic. In your mind, you did not make a move and thus, when someone else takes your place, say at a job you wanted, you then take it as rejection as the other person has taken what you thought was your place.

When your biggest fear is being vulnerable, you then take measures to try to make yourself less vulnerable. You avoid strong ties, you keep greatly to yourself and want to avoid revealing too much about yourself. In the end, this then makes you a perfect target for manipulators.

To get over your fears and make yourself mentally strong to not be manipulated, get out of your comfort zones, and do the thing you want to do anyway. If you want that job, but are afraid of rejection, go for it anyway. At worst, you will get a no. At best, you will learn that the world doesn't end afterward.

If you want to go out and meet new people, but are anxious, talk yourself into going anyway. It's something that you want to do, talk yourself into doing it.

This will take practice, and you will find yourself wishing to stop and curl further into yourself when you get the pinch of rejection. However, it takes practice, and knowing that rejection is not personal will go a long way in helping you build a powerful mind that can't be manipulated easily. When you make an effort to confront your fears, it builds your confidence.

When you have strong mental strength, you will be able to identify your emotions, acknowledge them, and deal with them without letting them control you. This will allow then to be able to tell when someone wants to make you feel inferior so that they may take advantage of you. Manipulators are charmers, and so, they will always want to be a step ahead. They could be doing this through sarcasm, or through trying to flatter you, have a very thrilling conversation with you as they load praise upon praise on you.

When you build your confidence and are more aware of yourself, you will catch on with these tactics and evade them.

So, go out there and do things. Become more knowledgeable, learn, or practice a new skill. If you have a talent, work on it until you become good at it. Take the time to talk and bond with close family and friends, go on holiday and have a jolly good time. Have yourself exposed to things that you are sensitive about so that you become a more rounded, confident person? The inner, vulnerable you will be grateful. Just don't overdo it.

Channel Positive Thoughts Frequently

What do you think of all day?

Or maybe I started ahead. I sit back and think. Are you aware of your daily thought patterns? What runs through your mind all day? Are these thoughts mostly positive or negative? Do you often feel more reassured afterward of drained?

When you are constantly in a cycle of negative, defeatist thoughts, you will often find that you begin acting more like a victim and thus feel as though things are beyond your control. However, as we have stated earlier, while there are things that are beyond your control, there are many more that are within your control. Focus on them instead.

Thoughts have a way of influencing our behavior, which then, in turn, influences how the world around interacts with the behavior. When you constantly are thinking negatively - 'oh, I will never amount to much, I am such a loser,' this then reflects on how you behave - as a loser, and thus, making you an easy target for someone that wants to use your vulnerability against you and for their gains.

Create a pattern where you identify negative thoughts and then put effort into channeling positive thoughts in its place. Negative thoughts will often leave you as the kind of person that someone could easily manipulate. Since you feel like you are useless, when someone comes with an external solution to what they lead you to believe is your problem, you will take the bait, in a bid to try to be more useful. Curb these thoughts.

When you find yourself thinking hard about your failures and weaknesses, pause, then, begin going through what you have achieved. Run yourself through your strengths, through your dreams.

This will require you to be constantly on the lookout to be aware of your thoughts. This will take practice, and you lose yourself on more times than one, but make a point of doing it anyway. Remember, one of the ways to build a strong mentality is to do things that make you anxious or afraid. So, keep tabs on those thoughts and your mind will thank you for it.

Have a Group of Positive People Around You

How do your friends react to your insecurities? And how do you react to theirs?

To build a strong mindset, you will need people. After all, as the saying goes, 'none of us is an island.' The thing is, characters and attitudes spread fast, and so, when we consistently hang around certain people, we become more likely to pick up on their habits and characters.

When you have friends, family, or acquaintances that are of positive influence to you, you will become more confident in who you are. You will feel alive, inspired. You will believe in yourself more and want to become better. This then creates room for you to work on improving yourself so that you do not become the dark stain in a pool of joy. This will then make you learn how to build a strong mentality. So, keep your circle full of inspiring and character-building people.

Create a Mentality of Thinking Critically and Ahead

when you build yourself enough to gain some confidence in yourself, then comes the part that will make you very hard to twist into the whims of the party trying to manipulate you.'

When you get to this point, you become aware that manipulation isn't often a straight cut as you have come to believe.

Thinking will require you to throw away the narrow-minded characteristic that comes with an emotional reaction to something that has been done to you.

Thinking will allow you to see manipulation in many places you never thought possible. When you know yourself, you will see manipulation in the advertisements and many other media. This is often a subtler kind of manipulation, meaning that to catch on it, you will need to understand the characteristics of manipulation - making you feel inadequate, selling your utopia, making you feel like an outsider.

In media and politics, manipulations are the name of the game. When you make a point of thinking critically, you will catch on the signs. You will know that, no, the product on the TV is not the key to your happiness. You will know that belonging to a popular political movement won't make your life better. You will see through the words and actions that are aimed, not at your mind, but at your heart, to twist you into making an emotional reaction - buying the product or joining the popular political movement, at the expense of your satisfaction. Did you need that item? Do your personal beliefs line up with the popular movement?

When political players and the media use manipulation, they will want you to think less and instead, act more. So, make a habit of combing through your thoughts with regards to what advertisers tell you through the media.

Thinking ahead will also allow you to spot inconsistencies in the behavior, utterances, and general demeanor of the person who wants to manipulate you. A manipulator will often want to use what you said against you. For that, they rely on your ability to doubt yourself and go back to the event, to question yourself. Once you do this, they then continue to feed into it, further reducing your ability to think, leading you down the path of an emotional reaction that would then benefit them and hurt you.

So, maintain tabs on what they said, keep yourself alert at all times around them. If the person is your spouse, let them know that you know what they are trying to do. Many will try to make your problem small as compared to theirs. They will blame you for their mistakes. They will then make communication difficult deliberately so that they can create a misunderstanding that will wear you down and make you act irrationally. Take a moment to think through before replying to them. Maintain your senses when you see that they are trying to pull their strings. This will then make them react even more desperately, in a bid to throw you off and push the blame back on you. Keep calm and think. If you find it hard, then go ahead and take a break.

With the media, this means that you will need to be comfortable in your own person. Be in touch with your core values. If your core values are on external things, then the media will easily manipulate you into buying things you don't need. Align your core values with intrinsic needs.

Conclusion

First of all, let me thank you, dear reader, for making it to the end of the book. It is with the best intentions to help you navigate through life with the mentality of a giant that we wrote this book. So, to recap, below are some of the topics we covered in brief descriptions.

We have covered dark psychology, which is seen as an art and science that is used to manipulate people and to control their minds. This type of mental control often involves a deep understanding of the human mind and psychology, and which is why governments and many people of influence have used it to give them an edge over you and me.

Speaking of governments, we covered on the secrets of dark psychology that the secret service uses in order to maintain their sense of intimidation and power, to create the aura of invincibility around them. Among the many techniques they use has often been the use of the black shaded to hide their eyes. This is to make it hard to know where one is looking at a particular time, meaning that if you are around them, you will likely behave yourself as you do not know who is watching.

We have also covered in part 2, on how you can become good at reading people through an understanding of their slightest emotional expressions, which we called micro-expressions, as well as reading body language. To know dark psychology, then understanding body language is critical.

This technique also included learning and knowing the personality types that most likely point one as a possible manipulator. These include Narcissism, shown by excess grandiosity and a lack of empathy; Machiavellianism, where one has no sense of morality; and psychopathy, where someone is often charming, but then becomes impulsive, selfish and without empathy.

We have also covered how NLP (Neuro-Linguistic Programming) has been used by advertisers and other people seeking to control people have used it to control people's mind. It is almost invisible to us now. We have looked at how people who have mastered this program can tell a lot about a person without any background detail and in a short period, thus making it a perfect tool for advertisers and confidence tricksters.

Then, we have also looked at the power of emotional manipulations, how it is used to make you feel either inadequate or not loved, and how this then makes you an easy target for further manipulation.

Finally, we have looked at the advanced ways in which you can build a powerful mind that will make you hard to manipulate. We started by making you aware of your emotional state of being and what within you makes you vulnerable and how you can build awareness with yourself to be mentally prepared. We have then looked at how you can build your confidence, which is often key towards a strong mentality, and therefore a powerful mind that will make you hard to manipulate. We have also looked at how facing your fears can help you develop the mental toughness to withstand manipulation and how you can rid yourself of negative thoughts that make you an easy target for manipulations.

So, thank you once more for enjoying this book!

9 781695 753280